Praise for *Trustworthy*

"Compassionate experience design sits squarely at the intersection of vulnerability, candor, and humility, and *Trustworthy* deftly delivers the roadmap to get you there."

KARA DEFRIAS Director of Experience Design, Obama White House

"Practical, generous, and filled with wisdom, this book can unlock your path to becoming trusted."

SETH GODIN author of *The Practice*

"In a world of misinformation and deep fakes, trust is a powerful asset. In *Trustworthy*, Margot Bloomstein identifies three core areas through which effective content strategy can fuel enduring trust. With examples from organizations spanning sectors and industries, Bloomstein provides valuable insight and tactical recommendations for business leaders seeking to engender trust in this era of digital transformation."

PERRY HEWITT Managing Director, Marketing and Technology, Brock Capital; former Chief Digital Officer, Harvard University

"*Trustworthy* brings together a cornucopia of real-life case studies and presents concrete examples of how to beat cynicism and build trust. It should be required reading for anyone interested in building a deeper, lasting rapport with their customers or audience."

CHRISTOPHER STREBEL Manager, Digital Content Experience, World Health Organization

"*Trustworthy* is more than a simple how-to for developing trust and establishing strong relationships with clients and audiences—it goes beyond this by illustrating *why* it is important to do these things. If you're trying to develop deeper and more meaningful engagements, read this book."

EDUARDO ORTIZ CEO, Coforma

"At long last, someone has exposed the truth about brands! Margot Bloomstein deftly reveals how branding must go beyond the infinite power grab for profits and begin to behave bravely in order to improve the world. In smart, elegant prose, Bloomstein explores how the responsibility of the corporation has evolved, and what it takes to create genuine trust between citizens and the companies they invite into their lives."

DEBBIE MILLMAN Host, *Design Matters*; Editorial Director, *Print* magazine; Chair, Masters in Branding, School of Visual Arts

"We live in a time where cynicism reigns. This book shines a light for those who want to build companies and brands that are honest, optimistic, enduring, and able to contribute real value to the world."

KHOI VINH Senior Director of Design, Adobe

"Just when everyone is failing everyone, Margot Bloomstein earns our confidence by exploding the myth that modern business is impersonal and shows us how good old risky-but-easy trust is the key to success in design, branding, marketing, and even life. *Trustworthy* has come just in time to make you feel human again."

SCOTT A. SANDAGE author of *Born Losers: A History of Failure in America*; Professor of History, Carnegie Mellon University

"Any organization striving to build community, engagement, and loyalty during a time of cynicism and economic uncertainty will benefit from the advice, insight, and concrete steps offered in *Trustworthy*."

MARCY KREVER Chief Communications Officer, American Montessori Society

"*Trustworthy* optimistically addresses the opportunities and challenges for building authentic connections with customers for brands of any size—especially growing ones."

RANDY J. HUNT Head of Design, Grab; former VP Design, Etsy

"When language is appropriate, it carries information, creates understanding, and can even create a feeling of familiarity. In turn, this level of intimately shared experience creates trust. With *Trustworthy*, Margot Bloomstein will help you craft language that can be innately understood and valued in this way, whether in business, marketing, civic life, or tech. And she'll inspire you do it with humility, grace, and confidence."

JOSH SILVERMAN Chair, Master of Design in Interaction Design program, California College of the Arts

"Whether you're building a new brand or overhauling your marketing, this practical and motivating guide will help you along the way. Margot Bloomstein offers a visionary perspective on building trust with your audience at a time when that trust is in short supply."

KATE KIEFER LEE Vice President of Communications and Corporate Affairs, Mailchimp

"With heart and smarts, *Trustworthy* provides the 'how' for brands that want to connect with hope and build genuine rapport."

SHARON ROWE CEO and founder, ECOBAGS

"Margot Bloomstein offers us not just direction for creating transactional trust, but also a model that will prompt brands and organizations to become a beacon of believability by putting forward their authentic values, most charismatic attributes, and unique characteristics. There's hardly an organization out there that wouldn't benefit from the guidance in this book."

KATE O'NEILL author of *Tech Humanist*; founder and CEO of KO Insights

Trustworthy

MARGOT BLOOMSTEIN

Trustworthy

HOW THE SMARTEST
BRANDS BEAT CYNICISM AND
BRIDGE THE TRUST GAP

PAGE TWO
BOOKS

Cataloguing in publication information is
available from Library and Archives Canada.
ISBN 978-1-989603-92-5 (hardcover)
ISBN 978-1-989603-93-2 (ebook)

Page Two
www.pagetwo.com

Edited by Jill Swenson and Amanda Lewis
Copyedited by Melissa Edwards
Proofread by Alison Strobel
Jacket design by Peter Cocking
Jacket illustration by Rich Woodall
Interior design by Setareh Ashrafologhalai
Printed and bound in Canada by Friesens
Distributed in Canada by Raincoast Books
Distributed in the US and internationally by
Publishers Group West, a division of Ingram

21 22 23 24 25   5 4 3 2 1

appropriateinc.com

For Clover, who makes me want to hope.
For Mike, who gives me reasons to hope.

Contents

CHAPTER 1   Introduction 1

(I)   **Voice** 11

CHAPTER 2   Communicate with consistency
across time and channels 17

CHAPTER 3   Educate with humility
and transparency 41

CHAPTER 4   Use plain language
to build confidence 59

(II)   **Volume** 81

CHAPTER 5   Share your work and
remove all doubt 89

CHAPTER 6   Say what you have to
say, then stop 109

CHAPTER 7   Balance fidelity and
abstraction to inform
beyond the facts 131

(III) **Vulnerability** 153

CHAPTER 8 Convene community
for collaborative creation 157

CHAPTER 9 Lean into the lessons
of what went wrong 173

CHAPTER 10 Vision for the future 203

Further reading 215

Interviews cited 217

Notes 221

Acknowledgments
and appreciation 239

Index 243

CHAPTER 1

Introduction

I DON'T believe you.

Oh, don't take it personally. I know you don't trust me, either. You probably don't believe most of what you hear; neither do I, and that's true for most people. Whether you work for a retail giant, government institution, or some other organization, you've probably noticed how so much of the marketing you see falls flat. Most messages don't motivate action. People just don't trust brands like they used to.

Consumers, citizens, and corporate buyers are feeling a sweeping, protective skepticism that undermines the delivery of information, products, and services in every sector of the economy. Can you blame them? Your audience has endured failures of leadership, inconsistent messaging, and deceptive practices from brands they thought they knew, in the halls of governments, and from public figures who used to offer a definitive perspective on the day's news. Cynicism takes root when people don't know who to trust and decide not to believe anything.

Everyone's just out to make a buck.
All politicians lie.
That's how they get you!

People turn away from experts, build affirming filter bubbles, and eventually turn inward—until they grow to distrust even their own gut instincts. They lose confidence in their ability to evaluate information and make good decisions. The world is an overwhelming place.

And that's exactly where you need to meet them. To regain your audience and their trust, you need to rebuild their confidence and empower them to make good decisions. Don't stoke their cynicism; that way isn't a path forward. Instead, help your audience help themselves by affirming their sense of hope. This is not easy work; it's far easier to appeal to your users' fear and anxiety. But it doesn't just keep *them* fearful, it keeps our *whole society* fearful—and angry, cynical, and stuck. Cynics look at the world as it is and say it's worse. But designers, writers, and marketers—as well as social media managers, CMOs, creative directors, people in corporate communications, user experience design, and content strategy—look at the world as it is and imagine it can be better.

If you're reading this book, you're perfectly positioned to make the world better through your involvement with content and design. Here's how.

Voice

Voice refers to the distinct personality that manifests visually and verbally in everything your brand does. Do you project a sense of tradition, or innovation? Are you witty and polished, or scrappy and creative? Your brand's voice helps your audience distinguish you from your competitors—but it also helps humanize your brand and elevate what you think is most important. It tells your audience who you are, how you are, and if you're someone they can trust.

By striking the right balance of consistency and novelty, jargon and plain language, your voice can teach people how to engage with your organization. Do you suffer growing pains? Learn how a consistent look-and-feel can help your company evolve over time, launch new products, and reach new channels—all while bringing your existing audience along with you. Hear from corporate communications and creative leadership at Mailchimp about how they avoided alienating small business owners as they grew into the marketing juggernaut they are today.

Ready to let your freak flag fly so your audience can find you? Before Mailchimp delivered monkey-powered email to a loyal customer base, Banana Republic took its quirky persona on safari and came back with a unique perspective—and an equally invested audience. Hear from the founding creative team who helped develop the brand's witty, literary voice and launch a surplus and safari outfitter through a travelogue that built rapport with a niche audience. Discover how building a visual and verbal language that's cohesive across channels can help your audience stick with you as your brand grows.

Then we'll go deeper into unpacking how to earn the confidence of your audience by engaging with humility and transparency. Learn how organizations as far-flung as the FBI and British sex toy retailer Lovehoney empower their audiences by openly sharing the limits of their expertise. Both organizations bring information design and content together to clarify the boundaries and limitations of institutional knowledge. Explore how elevating your weaknesses can offer a surprising opportunity to strengthen your brand—and the engagement of your audience.

Opening up about your brand's challenges and opportunities can bring you closer to your audience. But as they get to know you, do they encounter an impenetrable wall of jargon, thick copy blocks, and dense information design? Learn how to unpack the prose and empower your audience through the content design examples of the US National Institutes of Health and British National Health Service. Sit down with the people in these organizations who are leading the fight to integrate jargon in a way that educates rather than alienates— and take a page from the medical community that embraces plain language to better serve both its audience and clinicians. We'll pore through the NHS Service Manual and other guidelines to elevate the key lessons that transform even the most opaque organizations into trustworthy examples of authority and empowerment.

By embracing plain language, communicating with consistency, and engaging with humility, you'll discover tools to inspire renewed confidence in your audience. Your brand will reap the benefits—but your efforts will also serve a greater purpose. Your audience wants to feel more confident in themselves. By building a consistent, clear voice, you'll teach people to trust themselves again.

Volume

Voice addresses how you communicate; volume refers to *how much* you communicate, in both length and level of detail. How do you know how much to say on a topic? Do you prescribe blog posts and product descriptions in terms of character counts, or rather breadth of topics? Do image galleries need to convey the essence of a product or process, or the comprehensive experience? Brevity and bullets have ceded space to longform content, even on ecommerce sites—but that trend isn't a license to babble. So how do you determine how much content is enough? Explore examples that provide a clear answer: you've offered enough detail when your audience can make good decisions—and feel good about the decisions they make.

In some cases, detailed technical imagery and extensive product evaluations can foster the same sense of confidence and certainty as a prospective customer would find in doing the research themselves. But not all products, services, and circumstances allow for a test drive. Discover how sharing your work and raw data can give your audience greater faith in the process, your brand, and their own ability to make smart choices. With insight from the team at America's Test Kitchen, discover how more content can spell the difference between success for a niche audience and success—and satisfaction—for a broad range of users across a variety of platforms and channels.

More content isn't always more effective. Long descriptions, layered infographics, and multiple calls to action can overwhelm your audience and undermine their confidence, in both themselves and in you. Learn from the team at GOV.UK, who wrestled 75,000 pages about government services down to 3,000,[1] how to determine scope and focus the attention of your users—and your content contributors. Both will thank you for it.

Beyond looking at content in terms of length and level of detail, discover how abstraction can help empower your users and earn their trust. Look at any map and you'll see useful lies—a spin on reality that's helpful, valuable, and trustworthy. Maps are an example of abstraction, a technique that can help your organization move beyond overwhelming details about your services, products, or processes to information that's more actionable, relevant, and trustworthy. Explore how abstraction empowers doctor-patient communication, guides video production at Airbnb, and improves trust in the electoral process, all without compromising on authenticity. You'll also see how former congressional candidate Alexandra Chandler's work in the intelligence community sets a model for abstracting sensitive communication to the point of familiarity—valuable lessons for any organization that needs to navigate crisis communication, nuanced social issues, or challenging conversations with a thoughtful audience.

Vulnerability

Individually, a consistent voice and the appropriate volume are characteristics of good brand-driven content strategy and user-centered design. Those efforts unite to foster trust when you communicate by finding strength in vulnerability. Are you willing to risk criticism, ridicule, or rabid customers by revealing confounding challenges and hard truths? You make yourself vulnerable by engaging in that kind of transparency— but don't mistake it for weakness. The smartest brands grow stronger by owning their mistakes and embracing vulnerability. By operationalizing vulnerability, you expose your brand to criticism, input, and risk in the hope of reaping greater rewards. That exposure is humbling and can take down even the most hardened organizations—but it can also build community, loyalty, and champions of your brand. The tradeoff is enormous, and represents a huge shift in corporate communications.

Rather than project your brand as invincible, let's consider what you could gain in authenticity by bringing your community—critics included—behind the scenes. Learn how to embrace vulnerability by revealing the evolution of your brand and taking advantage of opportunities to prototype in public. Hear from the editorial team at TED and creative directors at *The New York Times* about convening community to inform a richer product. Then discover how serving your audience means forgetting everything you think you know about empathy and moving beyond arrogance to more compassionate experience design. We'll also dig into the process of cultivating community around the kitchen table with the lessons of Penzeys Spices. Putting a stake in the ground attracts critics and frustrates a few customers, but it can ultimately send your sales through the roof—even if you're a humble (and vocal) spice merchant.

It's risky for a brand to expose its inner workings and ethics, but it takes even more vulnerability and courage to acknowledge problems and be accountable to your clients.

The upside is that doing so can lead to innovation and growth. Your company is at its most vulnerable when critics, shareholders, customers, and the media clamor for an explanation and apology for bad behavior and mismanagement. In that moment, do you double down on defeat—or embrace the opportunity to evolve?

Smart brands seize the opportunity to build trust through a public accounting. They also don't shy away from acting with courage when circumstances demand difficult decisions but don't provide the cover of certainty or complete information. How do you navigate risk if your team doesn't have comprehensive information in a quickly evolving area? Learn from Dr. Sara Cody, whose leadership in the Bay Area's coronavirus response is a lesson in embracing risk and taking bold actions within the context of transparent communication and collaborative thinking. And when things go wrong, discover the value of apology in rebuilding rapport with your audience. Draw on examples that give us object lessons in accountability: a major malpractice insurer, a classic Kickstarter campaign, Old Navy, and video conferencing giant Zoom each offer lessons in how to communicate with courage, clarity, and compassion. It's in these moments of greatest vulnerability that your brand must rise above and outthink the greatest deterrent to trust: cynicism.

Accept this call to empower your audience. They're smart and hopeful—and they're desperate for the world around them to see that. As citizens and consumers, they want you to respect them, help them become smarter, and affirm their hope. You have the platform and tools to answer their call. Will you be so bold in your voice, supportive in your volume, and vulnerable in your own growth that your brand becomes the rare lifeline in a sea of cynics? In these pages, you have the tools, examples, and lessons to empower people through content and design. You'll hear from marketers, designers, writers, and leaders in healthcare, publishing, startups, apparel, government, retail, nonprofits, civic design, and academia with lessons you can bring to your team. Together, you can help your audience become more secure in a scary world and move through it not with certainty, but with confidence. Help them regain their trust in themselves and you'll regain their trust in your brand.

The world is counting on you—so let's go!

(I)

Voice

VOICE REFERS to the unique, identifiable personality that comes through in everything a company says or does. Your brand needs a voice for two reasons: first, it helps your audience distinguish your company, service, or institution from everyone else. You only matter if you're not generic; distinction helps you as much as it helps your audience. Second, voice humanizes your brand and gives it a perspective. Are you witty? Polished? Careful and conservative? Voice tells your audience who you are and how you are and gives them something to trust. You can't build trust if an audience doesn't know anything about you.

In marketing and brand development, voice is verbal as well as visual. It's the words in a message as well as the typeface or imagery used to convey them. Witty brands communicate that quality through bright colors, pithy sentences, and off-kilter photography. More conservative brands eschew all that. So who are you? And more importantly, does your audience know?

"Your voice is your company's personality," advise Nicole Fenton and Kate Kiefer Lee in their guide to writing for the web, *Nicely Said*.[1] While tone changes to fit the context and content of a message—we "tone things down" to convey gravity, or "shift the tone" to build enthusiasm—voice persists across platforms and contexts. To be distinct, it needs to be consistent. But some messages demand novelty or require your tone to shift and grow. As your organization evolves—perhaps expanding your mission, offering more services, or pivoting in a changing economy—you may need to seek out new styles or platforms for communication. In other cases, trust comes from the constraints you share or restraint you exercise.

Communication that's consistent, humble, and accessible builds trust by empowering your audience, demonstrating your care for them and earning their loyalty in return.

Nothing attracts attention like novelty—and nothing seems to nurture anxiety so much as the thought of being left behind. Often, it's a consistent voice that helps a brand bridge new products and tie together the roadmap for consumers. We crave and gladly pay for the next big thing, whether it's the latest release from Apple, the new season of a TV show, the next book by a favorite author, or a hot new sneaker from a beloved brand. The iPhone, *Stranger Things*, Louise Penny, and Vans are similar in that each knows their audience well enough to reward them with both novelty and consistency. As customers, we *don't* always want the next big thing. Sometimes we want familiarity, and to maintain what we know. We hold on to old phones not because technology is cyclical[2] but because they work, and nothing fits so well in a back pocket or purse. If you've ever bought a bag just because of how well your laptop fits inside, or purse because it holds your phone just right, you know the comfort of counting on things to work. When screens get bigger, technology can leave behind its most ardent fans. Yet brands want to evolve—due to market pressures, shareholder demands, and the pull of Moore's Law[3] compelling technology to be ever more powerful, faster, and fully featured—and it's on brands to bring their customers with them. Shared language, consistent branding, and thoughtful humility can go a long way toward maintaining customers' confidence and loyalty.

CHAPTER 2

Communicate with consistency across time and channels

GROWTH IS an awkward and often alienating experience—ask anyone who has a teenager at home, or anyone who *remembers* being a teenager at home. There are comforts and familiar touchpoints that you don't want to lose, but time marches on. With some luck and the support of people who know you, it carries you to even broader horizons.

For your business, growth may be a goal—but that doesn't mean it will be graceful. As you explore new opportunities, you risk alienating existing audiences. They worry, and with good reason. Will you forget about their needs? Send them to the back of the line as you focus customer service on newer products? Abandon the humor or responsiveness that endeared you to them when you were just starting out? What then?

Maintaining a voice that's consistent over time and across platforms is a demonstration of loyalty to your audience.

Come what may, you're invested in a conversation with them. Through a dependable verbal and visual personality, you help your audience understand who you are, who they are, and how you relate to each other. Do you see your customers as fellow entrepreneurs, and relate to them through imagery that features eye contact and first-person perspective? Do you play to their aspirations and offer them cultural references and perspectives they'll find nowhere else? Do you take the time to educate users, or to let them in on behind-the-scenes humor as a show of respect and mutual enthusiasm? These conscious choices help you find your audience and help them find you. As they get to know your brand through the subtle choices in what you communicate and how, you build rapport— and you also build something even more valuable. By showing loyalty to your audience, you earn their loyalty in return. That enduring connection is something no one wants to outgrow, as even the most independent teenager will attest.

Stay true to your roots—and water them

Kate Kiefer Lee reflects on the success and positioning of Mailchimp. When we spoke for this book, she was senior director of communications; as I write, she is now vice president of communications and corporate affairs. "We grew so much, so quickly," she tells me. "When we were smaller, customers felt more connected to us; we were a small company too!" Early in Mailchimp's growth, customers could easily get in touch with their CEO. As the company grew further, they had to scale and design ways of maintaining connection and building rapport. "In 2016, we made $400 million. As we've grown, we've made sure our message is 'we support small business, we were a small business too—we just grew.'" When Kate joined in 2010, there were about 30 employees. Within 10 years, the company grew to more than 1,200 employees. Today, the marketing automation platform serves more than 60% of the email marketing industry,[1] supporting more than 12 million customers.[2] While perhaps it's the classic "good problem to have," to say that Mailchimp needs to work to maintain their small business street cred is an understatement.

It's a common problem: when your company adds new services and builds success upon success, how do you continue to relate to legacy customers and clients who worry you've outgrown them? More importantly, how do you ensure they still relate to *you*? Together, Mailchimp's clients send more than 1 billion email messages every day—and above that fray, the company works to maintain a distinctive personality that aligns with the perspective and maturity of its brand and their customers, many of whom have grown their businesses alongside them. At Mailchimp, copywriters and designers make strategic choices to ensure consistency balances change over time. As the company rolls out new channels and services, they maintain the same familiar voice. Today's graphic language is simpler and uses a more mature color palette, but still finds footing in a bold, primary yellow. These choices take a cue from industrial designer Raymond Loewy's MAYA principle: by embracing the "most advanced, yet acceptable" elements, a brand can push its audience forward while it delivers products and experiences that are still welcome and familiar.[3]

Maintain familiarity as the brand evolves over time

"For a long time, businesses just used Mailchimp for email campaigns," Kate explains. Then Mailchimp rolled out a marketing CRM, Facebook ads, postcard printing and distribution, and more. The little email marketing company has long outgrown its category. "When we started adding channels and taking our product in a new direction, we had to make sure people knew we were still focusing on our core email product. One thing that helped: our voice and approach didn't change."

In Mailchimp's early days, its mascot, Freddie, popped up with jokes throughout the app. The company was known for being warm, charming, and supportive, and he fit in perfectly as the monkey making offbeat commentary about bananas in the error messages. "We try to be friendly, approachable, and fun," Kate says. "But Freddie took up a lot of space in the app—and didn't help people get their jobs done. He felt like a distraction, so we took him out and turned him into an icon. But we still try to be fun in a way that feels appropriate." As the audience grew familiar with Mailchimp's voice, they no longer needed interaction with a mascot as a reminder of what to expect in the experience. Mailchimp's editorial voice could drive home that message—using tone to shift appropriately for various contexts and products as needed.

"With our voice, we make sure we're always friendly, plainspoken, and informal," explains Mark DiCristina, senior director of brand marketing. "We always try to be on the level with our customers and meet them where they are. There's a difference between Mailchimp's voice and tone: we try to maintain a consistent voice, but we modulate our tone based

on the context and customer." When the context is more positive, content speaks to the user's excitement, curiosity, and
relief. When the context is more negative, it's attuned to the
user's frustration and stress.[4]

> **Positive:** "Nice work! Once you've sent your first email,
> you're officially part of the club."

> **Negative:** "We searched high and low but couldn't find what
> you're looking for. Let's find a better place for you to go."

When the purpose of the content is to entice and engage, it
can be more casual, witty, and self-aware. When the purpose
is to inform or reassure, it's more direct, specific, and concrete.
Consider how these different copy elements address the use
of ads on Facebook:

> **Enticing:** "Say hi. In an ad. Like this one."

> **Informing:** "If engagement drops too low, Facebook may
> cancel your ad. That sounds scary, but each audience is dif-
> ferent, so some trial and error is normal."

That shift is key to building rapport and welcoming customers into the product suite, no matter the level of their business
savvy or technical expertise. "If we're writing to a client who
doesn't know much about marketing automation, we're not
dumbing it down, but we're not using jargon, either," Mark
continues. "Whereas if we know we're speaking to an expert,
we remain informal and plainspoken but our vocabulary can
change. That helps us feel a bit closer than if we weren't paying as much attention." The difference is subtle but specific.

Beginners who are new to marketing get a different tone than experts who are more advanced marketers or agencies.

Beginners: "Add a personal touch to your marketing so it feels more like a 1-on-1 conversation."

Experts: "With Mailchimp's personalization tools, you can make your campaigns feel like 1-on-1 conversations."

In paying attention and shifting the tone, Mailchimp engages like any thoughtful conversationalist: it listens as much as it speaks.

Develop guidelines to offer guardrails for growth

Mailchimp's public and much-lauded style guide[5] details how to maintain a consistent voice across channels. It's that consistency that creates familiarity and helps customers feel comfortable even as they encounter new products—or take in bad news about their account or read crisis communications. To ensure customers can always feel secure relying on new products and the platform, the company invested in guidelines to help writers, designers, and others communicate consistently on behalf of the brand.

Mailchimp didn't always bring this kind of rigor to its brand—and perhaps no early-stage company should. The chaos and creative diversity of a new company brings it to a tipping point when it is no longer sustainable or economically sound to operate without the cohesion and efficiency of standardized practices. Fortunately, that creative primordial ooze also provides real-world AB testing, case examples, and the opportunity to determine best practices. A style guide is a phoenix shaking off the ashes—an investment in continuity and cohesion that arises from chaos.

"When I started in 2010, I was editing our website, guides, and customer service messaging—then I realized we didn't have anything serving as a baseline," Kate recalls. "So I started conducting a website content audit to figure out how we were communicating across different channels." From that audit, Kate began to catalogue and standardize editorial style, before moving on to voice and tone to create guidelines within the company's nascent content team. "We were responsible for all writing standards across customer support and every product team," she explains. To meet the challenges of so many touchpoints, she worked with company leadership and stakeholders to ensure that the natural voice and values of the company came through. But the company's growth posed a challenge for writers charged with consistency and for a broader team trying to maintain a high level of service.

"We want all our customers to feel like we still get it. So as we've grown, we've made sure our message is 'we support small business, we were a small business, we grew—and we didn't take outside money, so we can help you grow too.'"

That message comes to life through tactics in photography, typography, and phrasing. Though customers may not be able to easily reach the CEO anymore, the friendly and approachable voice and tone guidelines help writers communicate that same level of support. As Mailchimp has matured and left behind its more whimsical tactics, the voice remains fun and helpful. Consider more experimental channels like Freddie and Co.

i don't think i'll ever want to run my own business after this experiment.

FIGURE 2.1 A partnership announcement on Freddie and Co. and the inside scoop, shared by the store's manager on her blog.

Mailchimp launched this online store to better understand the experience of new small businesses taking their first foray into online engagement. It's accompanied by a blog that reveals the challenges of small business while describing the technical and legal nuances in simple words that unpack the baggage of terminology, jargon, and bureaucracy. Mailchimp engages as a friend that's there to help—and commiserate.

To build a voice that's friendly and informal, Mailchimp guides writers to use active voice, embrace contractions, and speak about the company in the first-person plural. The organization is built of people; they embrace a human, conversational style. "We're so excited to share a new service with you today" demonstrates ownership and engagement—which can feel risky, but actually breaks down any walls or pretense between the brand and its customers. To put "friendly" into practice, the guide also prompts people to "write positively," calling out phrasing that admonishes rather than instructs. Write "To get a donut, stand in line," not "You can't get a donut if you don't stand in line," notes the style guide. Not only does positive writing put customers in a positive mindset, it also biases them toward action. Positive writing can also be more efficient than copy that scolds. This is where marketing meets modern parenting: communication is designed to bolster, empower, and motivate the audience.

Create your own style guide to define the parameters of your brand's voice. What's in and what's out? Guidelines save time, money, and effort by helping writers more easily meet their goals out of the gate. They also help more people contribute to representing the brand through other types of corporate communication, such as a blog. Efficient and satisfying opportunities for contribution increase employees' loyalty and sense of purpose—and they also allow more people to be engaged with the brand as it evolves.

Mailchimp's style guide offers a playbook to a friendly, supportive voice. It allows the brand to evolve and transform like a contextually savvy social chameleon. But not everything is by the book—by design. Today, the company hires for the same qualities in customer support that it demonstrates in its brand, recruiting people who understand small business and ecommerce and can communicate with empathy and warmth.

"They go through great training. And really key: they have the freedom to connect and be friendly," Kate notes. Customer support associates lean on general guidelines to empower customers, maintain a friendly manner, and avoid phrasing that might inadvertently shift the full responsibility for user error to the customer. However, they engage in conversation and don't follow a prescribed script. "They have the freedom and flexibility to have real conversations with our customers. In support, we work a lot on talking points, but we don't script anything though. We try to leave room for natural, human voices. When we script everything, that's where we lose connection with customers." Much like Mailchimp's customers, support associates are empowered by supportive guidance and lots of examples for self-help.

Even if Freddie the monkey is less prominent, customers still find a strong visual connection with the brand as it matures. When products change and new services launch, it's key that the visual language still feels familiar and easy to understand. "We've grown up a little," Mark acknowledges. "Visually, behaviorally, in content. Freddie used to talk a lot.

There are still places now in the app that we're pretty loose, but we're not as goofy. There's still humor in the brand, but it's a little smarter, more of a wink. And the tone of the content and the visual design of the content evolved together."

Over a decade, the color palette remained yellow with orange and brown, though the largely yellow backgrounds have receded to a white field with cheery yellow callouts and fuss-free collage-like visual language. The "visual voice" of typography, color palette, illustration style, and white space reflects a brand that brings together multiple services and elevates representative voices that are cohesive. Like a family, the individual elements relate to each other, but they're not monolithic in presentation. Mailchimp traded monkey-centered illustration for more representative, human-interest photography, demonstrating a greater focus on customers than just the services and tools they provide to them.

"Given the baseline of the brand we had built, we had established an audience and a brand voice—and in the context of those things, simplifying the language and shifting to photography can help engender trust," says Mark. "But more than just that, one of the things that helps Mailchimp communicate successfully is we try to have a point of view come through. We don't just have photos; we have a certain way we take photos, always shooting our customers in a natural environment, looking at the camera and smiling. That point of view helps create a visually consistent and distinctive experience so people always know what to expect." In terms of new services, customers may not always know *what* Mailchimp will deliver—but visual and verbal style and tone ensure they always know *how* Mailchimp will deliver it.

Fly your flag so others can find you

Mailchimp has evolved over more than a decade by bringing customers along, visually and verbally. Their strategy echoes the early days of a mainstay American retailer, Banana Republic. In the early 1980s, the Banana Republic catalogue offered inspiration, stories, and clothing from off the beaten path, or at least the path understood by adventure-craving Americans. Before it was acquired by Gap Inc. and smoothed into a sober supplier of business casual classics, the surplus and safari outfitter-as-travelogue translated quirk into rapport with a loyal and equally quirky niche audience. Banana Republic was bold about who they were and how they were different, and by creating a unique voice they attracted a like-minded audience, eager to travel and curious about the world. The pages of their catalogue were filled with literary references and guest writers who presented the riches of the world for a largely white Western audience, while the editorial staff and designers established an in-crowd through those features. Jargon is an inside joke, and early Banana Republic went deep to develop a loyal following.

Acquisition and investment by the Gap allowed that rapport to flourish until the demands of corporate assimilation and cost-cutting became too much. By the late 1980s, Banana Republic as early customers knew it had disappeared. The culture around it had evolved too, becoming more aware of appropriation and colonialism and eager to diversify its perspectives. The language shifted, products and merchandising became more mainstream, and store design transformed from the land of elephants and airplanes to something more accessible to a broad and diverse customer base. Let's look at those early days and how they built a consistent, persistent voice across their channels, and how they found an audience that was so enthusiastic for the concept—all lessons that can give your organization a unique voice today.

"Mel and Patricia would go off on their adventures and come back, fulfilling fantasies for people stuck in their offices who weren't able to just leave and go on safari," explains Diana Landau, Banana Republic's catalogue editor from 1985 to 1987. "Mel and Patricia" were Mel and Patricia Ziegler, the founders of Banana Republic, who set the brand's vision for passion and curiosity, its unparalleled perspective in sourcing and retail, and its delightfully unique voice. The catalogue was a thick journal evocative of a back-pocket Moleskine. It featured sidebar dispatches from the Australian outback and Italian cafes alongside product reviews by the likes of poet Lawrence Ferlinghetti, aviation legend Kitty Banner, and JFK's press secretary, Pierre Salinger. On every page, every product told a vivid story, complete with meticulously detailed illustrations that didn't so much show the garment as much as the arms-akimbo confidence it could confer on the owner.

Break silos to create consistency

Whether you're beginning with a catalogue or building a startup through pitch decks, prototypes, and a trade show booth, a consistent voice doesn't just happen. Consistent brand presentation is the product of vision, design, strategy, and intent. Banana Republic grew from the vision of its founders, who worked together to set the initial look-and-feel and verbal style. They hired to build a team that could understand their vision and extend it across new channels, cultivate content from outside sources, and develop style guidelines so that other contributors could continue the process. Open communication and shared goals let that vision work across departments and specialties.

In many organizations, traditional silos get in the way of that collaborative process. Maybe sales reps don't share client feedback with the design team, and designers and copywriters sit on opposite ends of the building and rarely get in a room together. If that's the case, your audience isn't experiencing a cohesive brand. A content strategy driven by message architecture[6] addresses that challenge because it helps designers, product owners, writers, and user experience specialists all work from the same communication goals. A message architecture is a hierarchy of communication goals that reflect the brand's common vocabulary. You can also fight the challenge of siloed communication by ensuring that the people who develop the visual and verbal voice for your brand work together closely. Forget having design and content in separate parts of the office; when it's time to set a new foundation for a campaign, product, or company, they're better off together. By sharing the same space to nurture ideas and document them for the team, they can develop a consistent perspective on what makes your brand unique—and both contributors and customers will understand that vision much more clearly.

"We had a unified vision where words and pictures had to work together from the get-go," says Bonnie Dahan, Banana Republic's senior vice president of creative. "I translated the creative vision of our founders. Design and content germinated together. Mel came from the editorial world and had a strong idea of copy; Patricia was the illustrator and designer." Outside product reviews influenced the tone for internal copywriting. "We would send a vest or hat to a novelist or a writer from *The New Yorker*. They'd wear it and send us a review that set the tone. It was well-written, highbrow, and addressed to a reader who really took the time to read. It was succinct and well-crafted."

Bonnie describes a style of product copywriting that's now considered a luxury. Today, user reviews are typically the content that breaks with the corporate style, not the content that drives it. Banana Republic understood and respected its audience to such a degree that they took a distinctive approach: they cultivated user reviews from a hand-picked group that would help drive the editorial tone and overall corporate voice.

"Back then, you'd have people who'd wait for the catalogue to arrive and sit down to read it with a cup of coffee," muses Bonnie. "There's an obligation when you've set the bar with your customer to deliver good reading." Developing a consistent voice through catalogue communications contributed to demand for brick-and-mortar stores. Within several years they'd grown into a national chain. "The aspirational, adventurous mystique infused store signage, hangtags, every touchpoint of the customer journey."

Look the part to attract like-minded partners

The respect Banana Republic brought to its audience translated to an investment in detailed copy and outreach to explorers and literary giants. It also informed the trust that its customers could fill in some of the details for themselves, and the engagement with content made for a richer and more memorable experience. That belief shaped the choice to use illustrations instead of photography for the products.

Patricia Ziegler was previously an illustrator at the *San Francisco Chronicle* and knew the value of illustration in storytelling. "Think back all the way to illustrations in books when you were a child; there's something that speaks more to fantasy than photography can," Bonnie explains. "But it also allows you to picture yourself in it. Illustration allows for your imagination—and our whole brand was focused on engaging the customer's imagination! And let's face it: stories sell."

The storytelling component of the brand drove the wardrobing style of illustration. Without showing a face or body, the clothing appears to be modeled by a person—standing assertively, mid-stride, hands on hips. "We wanted to show the clothing with an attitude," explains Diana Landau. "The arms spread wide convey a sense of confidence and movement. We're striking out into the unknown, and here's what we're going to wear! But we also didn't want people looking at models; we wanted our customers to imagine themselves in the clothing." By offering people who might never go on safari—or wade through a military surplus store—the opportunity to imagine and dress the part, Banana Republic sold affordable fantasy. By defining the aspiration, the brand let its audience define themselves and relish the process.

Double down on all that makes you unique

Your organization can find focus and prioritize resources by doing the things that only you can do. Banana Republic found focus by prioritizing investments in the channels, creative work, and customer touchpoints that only they could get away with. Their customers were delighted with packaging shaped like animals, funny rhetorical asides hidden on the order form, and wardrobe travel tips available by phone. As your brand finds its voice, invest in helping it thrive and become more distinct. That effort helps your audience understand what makes you different from the competitors and why they remain loyal to you.

By defining itself consistently through visual and verbal choices and a cohesive visual language, Banana Republic helped its audience draw firm distinctions between themselves and the mainstream. The visual language did the same. "I tried to maintain the soft, well-worn qualities that spoke comfort. Realize this vintage merchandise was the antithesis of the stiff department store merchandise," explained Kevin Sarkki in a 2011 interview with *Abandoned Republic*, a fan site dedicated to cataloguing vintage Banana Republic content.[7] Kevin was the first staff illustrator Patricia Ziegler hired to take on the style she'd set. As department store aesthetics and mass-produced mall culture became more and more the norm in the 1980s, Banana Republic pushed against it. Stores featured life-sized elephant replicas among palm trees under a ceiling festooned with mosquito netting.

These elements set the store apart from other retail outlets, but also offered a backdrop for internal consistency within the brand itself. As Banana Republic grew, the cohesion helped with the development of new channels and touchpoints, like phone support, signage, and hangtags, which would always feel appropriate and familiar to the audience.

FIGURE 2.2 A Jeep appears to crash through the window at a Banana Republic store.

"We wanted the experience to feel like it was touched by human hands," says Bonnie. An immersive human experience— "always as travelers, never just tourists"—was at the heart of the brand, alongside adventure and fantasy. "In everything we did, we strived for authenticity, but we also went very far in whimsy and playfulness." If whimsy and authenticity seem to be at odds, Banana Republic figured out how to commit to both by pairing well-made, military surplus–grade products and guidance with the passion of adventure cohesively across all its contacts and connections.

Bonnie starts ticking off examples: "We asked, how can we delight the customer and astound the recipient even as they're packaging up their purchase? We created packaging in the shape of rhinos and bush planes! How could we help people buy shoes? We had a terrain tester so you could see what it would feel like to walk on cobblestones in Europe or sand on the beach!" Today, many outdoor retailers bring terrain simulators to the in-store experience. But no one had done it before Banana Republic. Their attention to detail and authenticity made it make sense.

Say a customer is trying to prepare for their next adventure, but they're unsure if they should pack cotton or wool. In 1985, Banana Republic launched the Climate Desk,[8] a toll-free number customers could call to learn more about a region as they prepared for a trip. "The Climate Desk offers up-to-the-minute worldwide information on daily and seasonal weather, current political situations, and local health precautions so you know what you're getting before you get there," explained *Backpacker Magazine* in its September 1986 issue.[9] Before that information was available to anyone at any time with just a few clicks and an internet connection, Banana Republic was already in the business of empowering their audience's dreams.

While the catalogue established the brand personality, the stores allowed that voice to become three-dimensional in the "total design" of an immersive retail experience that was the proving ground for today's cohesive multichannel experiences. "In one store, you might have a plane hanging from a ceiling or elephant charging through the wall; specific architecture allowed for creativity," Bonnie explains. "Everything was configured to let customers gasp when they came in and transport them into that world." Audio complemented the visuals, as stores featured a soundtrack of bird calls and hippo grunts.

While customers might know the brand from the catalogue, the in-store experience was special and designed to reflect a different context and the distractions of a moving audience. "We didn't just lift copy verbatim from the catalogues to the hangtags, but instead made sure everything the customer saw referenced the same vision," she says. Copy was shorter, typography was bolder—and showcased to catch the eye. "Messages a customer would see at the cash register might be framed in bamboo. For all the details, we had to think: was it Banana? That's true for any brand though. One misstep can undermine the brand and take it into the world of parody."

Parody might be the most painful punishment, and inconsistency can degrade trust—but so can the exclusionary language of racism, however inadvertent. A brand's tone clarifies who's in its audience, but also who's not. More inclusive language creates trust and builds rapport with a broader audience. Banana Republic's florid copy celebrated colonialist attitudes and attire in equal measure. Today, we can cringe at the Safari Dress: "If Lord Kitchener had been a Lady, she would have worn this dress while routing the Mahdists and bringing the Sudan back into the Imperial fold." Yet they aimed to elevate the clothing and its construction, not just romanticize its roots or the story of discovering it. A few years later, competitor J. Peterman caught far more scorn and mockery for their ostentatious and oblivious copy. The Owner's Hat,[10] made of woven straw, offers a fair representation of the tone: "Some of us work on the plantation. Some of us own the plantation. Facts are facts. This hat is for those who own the plantation." Even at the time it was published, the description raised eyebrows for such casual, flippant allusions to slavery in marketing copy.

Today, vintage Banana Republic still inspires a passionate community of fans who snatch up old catalogues, print collateral, and eBayed trench coats. These followers value the brand in part because it always valued them, allowing room for customers' imagination in the illustration, literary passages, and lush details of the designed experience.

Nancy Friedman, Banana Republic's former editorial director, offers a nuanced perspective on loyalty and the brand's contrast with J. Peterman: "The J. Peterman Company was so centered on the character of J. Peterman; it was so much first-person singular," she recalls. "It was a little more rarefied. They didn't have stores, and there was a little more mystique around this one guy. Who was he? We were a little more accessible—and we were plural." Copy established rapport on a stylistic level by speaking in the first-person plural and focusing on the product: "We've revived this first-rate fabric" which is "rugged enough to repel mosquitos and tropical vegetation."

In contrast, the J. Peterman catalogue wrote in the singular and focused on the mystique of the character. Both brands offered storytelling and spoke of adventure, but one built up the reader as a fellow traveler keen to build wisdom and a practical wardrobe.

That respect echoes the real-world experience around early sales. "In the Bay Area, we had a really local following," Nancy explains. "In Mill Valley, where the Zieglers lived and opened the first store, there was a human connection that rippled out.

Peterman was more from on high and more elegant, offering velvet smoking jackets and different aspirations. We were more gritty."

"We were really aware of being travelers, not tourists... we didn't want to condescend or demean; we wanted to be respectful," she continues. "The Lonely Planet guidebooks were our bibles. Not to say how to do it on $5 a day or to say 'ooh, they're so different and exotic,' because we hated *exotic*. We were saying, this is our world, let's embrace it. We're smart and eager to experience things."

The early era of Banana Republic balanced respect for the world with respect for its starry-eyed customers—and respect for the brand and the team that brought it to life. Like Mailchimp, Banana Republic let an expansive brand thrive not by scripting every phrase and dictating a narrow visual system but by articulating a clear vision and committing to serve that message architecture with dedication to the details. Both brands hold on loosely to allow for growth; rather than monolithic and uniform, they are cohesive and all the more human for it.

Voice can be a slippery thing, especially as your organization evolves over time. Within that evolution, consistency over time helps both your audience and your organization. As you grow to offer other services or expand into new channels, your attention to familiar topics, editorial and illustration style, and typography assure your audience that you haven't forgotten who you are—or who they are. As Mailchimp demonstrates, clear guidelines can define the playing field and rules so contributors know how to communicate and get it right the first time. Banana Republic offers further evidence

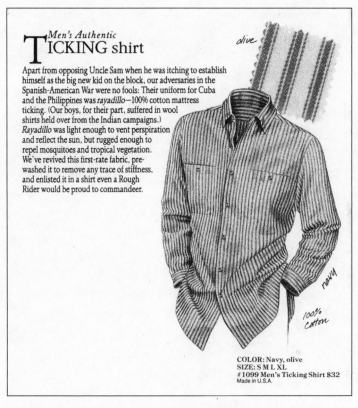

Men's Authentic

TICKING shirt

Apart from opposing Uncle Sam when he was itching to establish himself as the big new kid on the block, our adversaries in the Spanish-American War were no fools: Their uniform for Cuba and the Philippines was *rayadillo*—100% cotton mattress ticking. (Our boys, for their part, suffered in wool shirts held over from the Indian campaigns.) *Rayadillo* was light enough to vent perspiration and reflect the sun, but rugged enough to repel mosquitoes and tropical vegetation. We've revived this first-rate fabric, pre-washed it to remove any trace of stiffness, and enlisted it in a shirt even a Rough Rider would be proud to commandeer.

olive

navy

100% cotton

COLOR: Navy, olive
SIZE: S M L XL
#1099 Men's Ticking Shirt $32
Made in U.S.A.

FIGURE 2.3 The "Men's Authentic Ticking Shirt" from Banana Republic's Fall 1987 catalogue.

of how a brand can thrive by setting a clear vision for what it is, and what it's not—and that vision attracts people who revel in it.

Find your audience, find your new hires, and help them find you. With a consistent and distinct voice, you'll build their confidence and earn their trust along the way.

CHAPTER 3

Educate with humility and transparency

GROWTH IS a challenge that tests both our means and our messaging. If you handle it with humility and transparency, your audience will learn what to expect, and to recognize where things are still very much a work in progress. This effort can take many forms. To nurture an idea into fruition requires means: money, talent, and labor. But it also demands the right messaging: a clear vision that leaders can articulate with vigor, whether they're motivating potential investors or prospective hires.

Your brand's voice needs to convey your strategy for success and opportunities for audience participation. If you project too much confidence, you run the risk of sidelining would-be contributors who could bring valuable experience to the table. Arrogance is impenetrable. If you oversell the value of a product or service, you could lose the people it fails to serve—maybe forever, even as you add features and improve functionality. It can be frustrating to realize you've lost your audience; it's the plea for second chances behind signs like "Under new management!" and "Think you know us? Try us again!"

Brands that communicate with transparency build rapport with their audiences, but it's not without risk and nuance. Humility can mitigate that risk. Humble but confident communication can help you speak with authority about the depth of your organization's knowledge, research, or expertise, without pretending to wield a breadth of expertise that just isn't there. It takes humility to say, "We've decided to prioritize these features—but if you want something different, we recommend you look to one of our competitors." In not so many words, that's precisely the message conveyed by many successful single-product companies that choose to specialize in one corner of the market.

That authoritative combination of transparency and humility particularly pays off when you build a reputation for doing one thing and doing it well. When you want functional, comfortable, buoyant shoes, look at Crocs. But don't look to them for a dress shoe. Want a great grater? Turn to Microplane, manufacturer of rasps for hard cheese, callused feet, and rough wood. Just don't assume you can outfit your entire woodworking shop, bathroom vanity, or kitchen there. In the market for headphones? Consider Koss, the Milwaukee-based manufacturer that developed the first high-fidelity stereo headphones. They tried diversifying into other areas, but only lost money. So they went back to just developing headphones, and went on to make the first that delivered all 10 octaves audible to human ears. Later, they developed the first Wi-Fi headphones. Today, among mid-priced headphone makers, they are widely regarded as the best, and remain focused there with ads that emphasize their product as the easy, obvious choice.

FIGURE 3.1 Koss ads are usually warm, simple, and timely. This 1972 ad underscores the product's ease of use: if you want to enjoy music, they just work.

By being up front about what they do well and what they don't, brands that communicate with humility define their boundaries. They're clear on the limits of their knowledge, the features a product supports, and the services they're still fleshing out. But why do boundaries matter, especially in capitalist societies where businesses and their shareholders crow for constant growth? Here's why: by defining boundaries clearly and consistently—laying out our strengths as well as areas outside our purview—we let our audiences know what to expect and where we can deliver well and consistently.

Define boundaries to empower and educate your audience

"Men don't have the vocabulary to describe the sort of toy they want," says Matthew Curry, former head of ecommerce at Lovehoney, a British retailer of erotic toys and clothing. Lovehoney aims to engage customers on their terms—and in their terminology. They bring clarity and transparency to an industry that's known for shrouding product specs in cursory descriptions, salacious photography, and salty euphemisms.

Lovehoney embraces their digital chat feature and uses it to speak clearly about what they know—toy design, materials, features, pricing, user reviews—and openly about what they don't, all in service of educating prospective customers. The boundaries of the chatbot's capabilities are clear, and users are prompted to go to the product pages or to engage a live person if they hit those boundaries. But before that, the conversational tone and correct vocabulary educate and empower users—no salacious euphemisms necessary.

By using the correct words for product types and materials, Lovehoney is giving their customers the vocabulary and confidence to ask for precisely what they want. While women search for sex toys on a variety of form factors and brand names, "there are no commonly used words to describe male toys," Matthew continues. "So we started thinking about guided shopping experiences. Maybe if we could ask the visitor a few questions, we could nail down the sort of thing they were after."

The resulting back-and-forth conversation looks a lot like a common practice of many successful offline retailers. Consultative sales, in which the associate or account manager asks questions of the customer to clarify their needs and help them understand their options, can be educational and empowering. When someone shops for kitchen appliances, they gain knowledge about the range of products that might suit their needs, and the features that might be most pleasing. Need a new stove? Gas, electric, or induction? You're not sure, but you're really keen on a smooth cooktop and the ability to maintain a precise temperature? Okay, let's talk more about induction. Looking for something inexpensive for everyday use, or something suited for entertaining? Will one large burner make all the difference for preparing big pots of soup every few days—or is that overkill for a small family that lives in a warm climate?

Appliance shopping can be daunting, in part due to the number of brands, features, and retailers that crowd the space. The knowledge consumers gain as they narrow down their options helps them feel more confident about making a purchase, but the voice of the retailer and sales associate shapes the experience too. If they're too pushy and assertive, they can quickly turn the customer's growing confidence into resentment. But what if the associate creates space for the consumer to learn at their own pace? What if they periodically assess whether the consumer still needs help, perhaps by noticing body language or by directly asking? Then they are replacing arrogance with humility. In exchange for empowerment, they earn the customer's trust.

Consultative sales are rare in the sex toy industry, but Lovehoney is changing that approach. In 2017, Lovehoney launched its first guided shopping "wizard." The step-by-step question-and-answer conversation tapped the company's broad product content and presented it in the framework of a discreet, non-judgmental chatbot. It was helpful, but not presumptuous. The chatbot helped users understand their options, narrow their choices, and make more informed decisions, all while peppering the process with questions to confirm it was still offering value and not being a nuisance.

Guided shopping wizards drive many experiences: they help consumers make better choices about home audio systems, baby shower registries, and even political candidates. Users narrow down their options and get a sense of the process, helping them to filter personalized, optimized recommendations— build the best car for you! put together the baby registry that's everything you want, nothing you don't!—from the vast world beyond it. By swapping jargon for more consultative conversational semantics, Lovehoney tries to help its visitors make better choices and feel comfortable and confident in the information they find in what is often a secretive, furtive search. The chatbot engages users in conversation to help them feel smart and confident in their purchase of a toy.

"We're testing it to understand the tone and level of detail customers expect," Matthew explains. "We want to keep it colloquial, to match our customer service tone of voice." In the public beta-launch, that tone was cheeky, jovial, and adolescent, which belies Lovehoney's extensive product knowledge and analysis that sets them apart from competitors. But consistency in voice across social media channels, the website, and phone support may prove to be a more reassuring factor to build trust. Sentence case, modern style, and conversational phrasing help users share their needs and get friendly product recommendations.

That approachable tone wasn't always there. At first, Lovehoney's chatbot, called Wankbot, sounded more formal. It used language that was both foreign to the brand and off-putting to customers. "The alpha version was a bit medical and sterile, so we've swung the other way," Matthew notes. By the time the beta launched, Wankbot offered a businesslike but convivial tone that couched supporting information in its structured search. "How much are you planning to spend on this new toy? The more you spend, the better it'll feel because more expensive toys are made from real-feel material," advised the chatbot. Later responses to a more cost-conscious shopper maintain the level of detail: "Cool. The best thing you could buy is one of these. Check them out—all these are less than twenty quid." The experience reassures a customer with colloquial affirmations ("cool") and short but educational interjections so that they leave feeling both smart and confident that they got the best personalized recommendations.

Wankbot sounds smart, savvy, and supportive—without slipping into condescension. It reflects the language the customer uses in their product searches, but doesn't aim to sound too human. The brand is humble and transparent about sharing the limitations of a chatbot. Rather than overplay its product knowledge, it offers users frequent ways to exit the conversation. The final exchange in a Wankbot session acknowledges that the tool is still in beta: "[This is] our first foray into sort-of-automated chat-based help. What did you think?" Shoppers have the opportunity for feedback, choosing among "Helpful," "Fun but not helpful," "Annoyingly pointless," and "Meh." Lovehoney prides itself on an open, accessible brand and user experience. Their transparent approach to "prototyping in public" is a testament to these values.

Lovehoney launched Wankbot to an audience of men shopping for themselves. They learned from the feedback and next launched a gifting chatbot to target men shopping for women. Vibebot offers questions in a tree-and-branch "choose your own adventure" model to help customers get product recommendations based on their knowledge—or lack thereof—of features, budget, and partner preferences. The bot doesn't resort to caveats, but it does launch with language that clarifies its purpose and that it's a work in progress:

> Hi hi hi! Thank you for trying out our experimental Vibebot :-) Vibebot is designed to help men choose a vibrator for their female partner, girlfriend, wife, mistress, friend-with-benefits... we hope you find it useful—do let us know at the end—thanks!

Smiley emojis and words like "experimental" are disarming by design. They intentionally undercut the clear, purposeful appearance of the interface. The look-and-feel uses an uncluttered background that puts the chat window right in the middle of the screen, rather than relegating it to a sidebar or separate pop-up window; on other sites, those chat features can be crowded with partner branding or evoke old text-based instant messaging windows. The Lovehoney chatbot offers more white space around the typography, and gives the text more room to breathe.

By pairing it with an informal reminder that the recommendation engine is still experimental, Lovehoney communicates

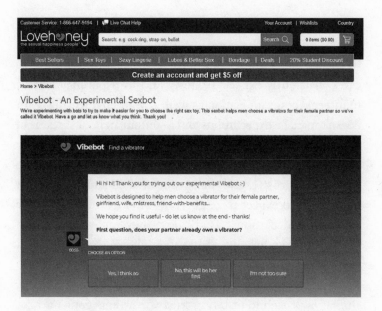

FIGURE 3.2 Simple language and short sentences take center stage in the Lovehoney chatbot.

that, as robust as the interface may look, users shouldn't expect perfection. By speaking of the company in the first person and referring separately to Vibebot, Lovehoney creates some distance that allows the user to give feedback on the chat experience without necessarily coloring their perception of the retailer.

Expose weaknesses to foster confidence

Organizations maintain the authority of their expertise by clarifying the boundaries of that expertise. Lovehoney isn't *admitting* what it doesn't know or what content isn't yet supported by its chatbot; it's *leading* with that information to ensure users know what level of detail and quality they can consistently expect. Honesty and transparency extend to internal communication as well. If your engineering team doesn't manage expectations and maintain an honest status of features or content under development, marketing can't hope to keep consumers apprised of what's coming down the pipeline. To earn trust, brands must educate their audiences, teach them what to expect through every interaction, and deliver on those expectations. That's how they renew confidence in their own knowledge and in their choice to interact with those organizations.

Miles away from Lovehoney, the FBI offers a strikingly similar approach to fostering trustworthy engagement. Like Lovehoney, the FBI presents an interface to invite engagement and manage expectations. Not surprisingly, the content is different, though the challenge is similar. The FBI aggregates massive amounts of information and data and needs to make it accessible to help its audience make better decisions— and feel confident in the decisions they make. And as in more design-driven cultures, the FBI wrestles with the challenge to be useful, usable, and desirable. In 2015, when crime statistics data were siloed, slow to publish, and often incomplete, former FBI director James Comey raised a mandate: "We need more transparency and accountability in law enforcement and better, more informed conversations about crime."[1] Information design and content strategy act on that edict, drawing from the crime statistics database.

Going beyond identification of the boundaries of its knowledge, the FBI gets out ahead of critics to spotlight weaknesses
in its data and explain why it's still valuable and worth using,
contributing to, and trusting. This is a conversation around
crime data, but it's equally relevant to anyone who works in
community management, product reviews, or the integration
of manufacturer and user-generated content.

"The FBI has been collecting data from federal, state, local,
university, and tribal law enforcement agencies for decades,"
explains Nicole Fenton, former head of content design at
18F in the General Services Administration and co-author
of *Nicely Said*, a guide to writing more clearly.[2] "We built an
application programming interface (API) and data visualiza-
tion site where journalists, criminologists, law enforcement
officers, and the general public can explore by crime type,
agency, and location," she says. "So, we tried to explain it in
terms any grown human can understand." With that goal in
mind, the Crime Data Explorer welcomes its users with a
calm color palette and a frank mission statement: "Improving
access to crime data." Headings are official but not officious,
and set in sentence case. Simple, familiar verbs clarify the
three main options—and levels of detail—that were initially
available to users who want to interact with the data and
study trends: "view trends," "download bulk datasets," and
"access the Crime Data API." Further down the page, users
see an invitation to "use our data in your project," with more
information about the provenance and limitations of open
data and brief definitions to describe each dataset. The clear-
eyed tone of voice complements a palette of crimson, white,

and slate blue, a more muted and mature version of the red, white, and blue that floods most US government websites.

"We took a shot at writing in a conversational way to see if people could understand what we needed them to know," Nicole continues. Like consumer brands that have found value in shifting to a tone that's conversational but not glib, the FBI created a voice that makes its information more accessible and usable. As an FBI statistician eyed new phrasing for accuracy, "persons" became "people," "ethnic origin" became the colloquial "ethnicity," and "LEAs" were spelled out as "law enforcement agencies." That way, they avoided jargon that might slow down some audiences or make the content seem more officious than useful.

These style choices are not without debate. The language of policing and crime statistics themselves can obscure racial profiling, foster incorrect assumptions, and perpetuate systemic injustice. Jargon itself has a negative connotation, but in many cases it can help educate readers, and expand their technical vocabulary and ability to sift facts from fiction. Familiar acronyms—like FBI for the Federal Bureau of Investigation—can convey the imprimatur of official status, and technical terminology can help a brand establish rapport, particularly if prospective customers want to gain product knowledge. The Crime Data Explorer looks beyond education to usage and empowerment. Jargon puts up a wall for some people, so to engage the greatest range of users in their research, the FBI trades rapport with a limited group for common language and access for all by spelling out acronyms in first usage in any given section on the site. Instead of throwing around SRS and NIBRS, many sections reference the Summary Reporting System and National Incident-Based Reporting System. The organization elevates the subject matter without the stiff-lipped, self-important tone that often accompanies crime reporting. The data gains the clear-eyed connotation of academic research—and the whiff of objectivity and rigor that accompanies it.

While those qualities engender trust, they also run the risk of making the database seem like it contains greater depth than it actually offers. That's where deft, timely content design and assertive graphic language balance out the tone. Content design is the practice of analyzing users' information needs and habits to determine and deploy the most appropriate content types—whether that means a chart, illustration, infographic, pull quote, or copy block. Graphic language refers to the gestalt of all the visual elements that convey the essence of a brand: typography, color, density, style of photography, and more. Consider how IKEA conveys enormity without intimidation: large, simple typography and flat areas of solid blue and yellow appear on large stores and unending displays, equally dense catalogues, and print collateral to communicate overwhelming scale made accessible. At Uniqlo, the graphic language is more firmly rooted in modern Japanese design. The details are few, and those that remain are polished. These traits come through in narrow sans-serif typography, uncluttered signage, ample white space on the website, and a streamlined, muted color palette in the apparel itself. Those elements combine to communicate simplicity, minimalism, and optimization.

At the FBI Crime Data Explorer, the design of data and supporting messaging work together to convey the richness of information but limits of its depth. The graphic language asserts that it is voluminous, designed to be used, but constrained in areas. It aims to engage users, but not fail them and potentially lose their trust. Large dropdown menus under bold text titles offer users a sense of control and convey how easy it is to use data. But equally large headings call out footnotes to explain the limitations and shortcomings of data. Extensive copy blocks show at a glance that there may be many exceptions or caveats that go along with it.

"The problem with the FBI Crime Data Explorer is that it's not comprehensive," Nicole cautions. The nature of self-reporting is that the data has gaps—but those gaps don't diminish the data's value. The FBI doesn't want perfect to become the enemy of good. "It's up to individual agencies to share with the FBI. So our job is to make the caveats as clear as possible in the relevant context. This is the most comprehensive crime data we have, and our hope is that by making it more visible and accessible, more law enforcement officers and agencies will want to share their data," says Nicole. "Good enough" isn't the message here either; the FBI wants agencies to appreciate using the data so much that they see the value of contributing to it as well.

In balancing between selling the value and conveying the limitations of the database, the FBI and Lovehoney wrangle similar challenges. Just as the tone in a chatbot can cause shoppers to draw incorrect conclusions about a product range, the presentation of information in diagrams can oversell the accuracy of data or cause users to misread its meaning. The FBI addresses this issue visually and verbally to ensure users find information valuable but not misleading.

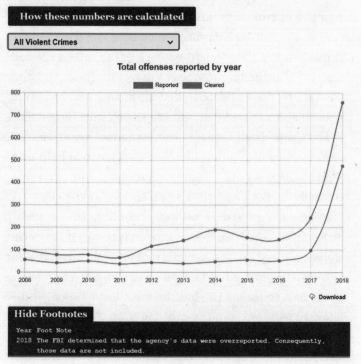

FIGURE 3.3 Crime reporting in Clark County, Nevada, gains context with a footnote. The FBI chose to remove redundant information after they determined it was overreported.

"Initially, our charts showed bubbles that made them feel more precise than they were," Nicole explains. "But the data has a lot of holes; just because the number of incidents is lower in a given year doesn't necessarily mean the crime rate is lower—just that a lower number was reported." Inconsistent reporting can create confusion too. For example, users could see Orlando's 2016 crime surge and suspect drug trafficking or an uptick in gun sales—and forget a single incident: the horrific Pulse nightclub shooting, which is included in the year's homicide totals. They might notice a crime spike in Nevada in 2018—but the footnote tells the rest of the story. Crime didn't surge; the FBI determined the jurisdiction had overreported it and removed that year's reporting from the database.

The Crime Data Explorer uses dynamic, integrated footnotes to put information like that in context to help users avoid giving wings to misinterpretations. Assumptions can be speedy, slippery, and insidious. If someone makes incorrect inferences from the data without consulting the context in the footnotes, they can fuel misunderstanding. If they bring inferences based on false assumptions into other research, the errors can be repeated and magnified. Later, when they realize errors, or a colleague catches the misinterpretation, embarrassment can lead some to cast doubt on the entire system. The FBI's investment in contextually appropriate instructional copy helps its users feel smarter and more confident. But it also helps the institution safeguard its own reputation, values, and integrity.

With a more familiar tone, jargon-free language, and helpful design elements, the crime data gains relevance without sacrificing gravity or accuracy. People can use it more easily and better understand context to interpret and act on it. Access to large volumes of data can build trust. The FBI taps into this practice by letting users sift raw data to draw their own conclusions. In some cultures and countries, crime data is squirreled away by the government to be sanitized and euphemized until it's fit for public consumption. Here, the FBI honors their audiences by trusting them to use the data wisely, which in turn fosters trust in the FBI.

Lovehoney, the FBI, and a broad range of other institutions create and sustain success by embracing a bold gamble: they trade secrecy for trust. Rather than trying to keep weaknesses or limitations a secret, they choose to inform the audience, and remind them where appropriate. Boundaries help to set expectations for the limits of a product or service. More importantly, when organizations clearly state the boundaries or limitations, they also set the expectation that users can count on an honest, forthright experience. You further bolster these expectations by calling out weaknesses before they attract critics or surprise customers. The payoff benefits both brand and audience alike, and reveals a fundamental truth about building real, lasting, profitable relationships with your customers, constituents, and colleagues: education is key to empowerment. Organizations that nurture their users' self-confidence in turn gain confidence from their audiences—in the form of time on site, contributions to the community, and ever-increasing trust.

CHAPTER 4

Use plain language to build confidence

YOUR ORGANIZATION can earn trust by leading with a clear message: "Here's what we do, and do well." The FBI and Lovehoney demonstrate the value of also being up front and humble about what you don't do. More than that, though, they earn respect by not cloaking that communication in words that are more complex than necessary. Humility delivered with simplicity builds confidence.

Thoreau advised us to "simplify, simplify."[1] At both the US National Institutes of Health and British National Health Service (NHS), writers and designers aim to do him one better. They simplify information, but they also make the data they present actionable. By presenting technical guidance and complex concepts in plain language and clear information design, they make the abstract concrete. Topics that might have been emotionally fraught become manageable. Users sift through content to gain knowledge—and with it, they gain the confidence to manage day-to-day self-care and consider more cutting-edge medicine. They're also empowered to take on something even more risky: in the face of illness, they gain the confidence to hope.

Hope, confidence, and trust are noble pursuits—so why do we put barriers around them? In part, we avoid direct communication because it's a form of risk aversion. Long sentences and legalese can feel safe, especially in industries where that style is the standard. Just as centuries of caked-on mud can protect ancient amphorae, the thick language of passive voice and nominalizations are protective, familiar, and comfortable. It's only by stripping away calcified language and cleaning off that mud that we unearth specific and clear communication.

The NHS uses active voice rather than passive voice to be clear, concise, and empowering. You can't drive action without using active voice. Active voice clarifies responsibility: it says who does what to whom by making the agent or actor the subject of the sentence. Passive voice hides that responsibility, and often uses more words and a formal tone to do so. It helps the writer (and often the subject) avoid risk because it hides the person who's supposed to be performing the action. Consider the difference:

Passive: Your appointment had to be rescheduled. The procedure will be explained by your doctor. Any questions should be asked at that point.

Active: The office coordinator had to reschedule your appointment. Your doctor will explain the procedure. You should ask any questions at that point.

Some topics require a formal tone. But rather than dressing up a concept in the stuffy sentence structure of passive voice, first take a look at your diction, or word choice. More formal, technical, or traditional terms can communicate the gravity of a situation.

> **Passive:** A serious allergic reaction could be happening and a doctor needs to be seen immediately.

> **Active:** You could be having a serious allergic reaction and need to see a doctor immediately.

Nominalizations are another way we bring more formality into our writing. Nominalization is the process of making a noun from a verb or adjective to describe a process or concept. In that way, "nominalization" is a nominalization itself: it replaces an action (nominalize) with an inert noun and adds length and formality in the process. NHS unpacks those nominalizations to get back to plain language:

> **Nominalization:** The test results are an indication of an infection.

> **Verb-driven phrase:** The test results indicate you are infected.

> **Nominalization:** Catheterization will be required.

> **Verb-driven phrase:** Your doctor will need to catheterize you.

Visual communication also requires effort and attention to be clear and useful. Stock photography can seem clichéd because it's often familiar, safe, and lazy. It doesn't test the boundaries of illustrating ideas with images that are specific to the topic, or say anything new in a manner that would require approval from a legal team. Visual communication also comes off as lazy when we attempt to cover all the bases: rather than refine an infographic down to actionable information, we merely present data without abstraction or perspective. In both cases, specificity takes effort: we are doing the work so our users don't have to. Like sculpture, visual information is complete when there's nothing more to take away. We can always add clarifying detail, but the most complex topics deserve communication that is as simple as possible, but no simpler, to use Einstein's maxim.[2] Let your audience gain confidence in ideas illustrated by clear and concise images, rather than get baffled by efforts to dress them up.

Speak simply to help people help themselves

"The government always need to be building trust," notes Nicole Fenton. "People don't inherently trust governments, and don't always understand that the government is made of people." In her time as the head of content design at the US General Services Administration, Nicole saw the challenges of this mindset, as well as the foibles of communication shaped as much by people as by processes. Along with the FBI's Crime Data Explorer, Nicole's portfolio also included more internally focused efforts like the redesign of PlainLanguage.gov, the website of The Plain Language Action and Information Network (PLAIN). PLAIN is a group of federal employees who advocate for the use of straightforward and simple language in government communications. They believe clear communication better serves the public—all while it saves the government time and saves taxpayers money.

Nicole combined user research, content testing, content design, and content strategy to develop new ways of better serving the public through both published content and the internal processes that guide publishing.

"We're mostly concerned with getting people clear information to make decisions," she explains. Case in point: ClinicalTrials.gov is the front end to a registry of clinical studies being conducted all around the world. While the National Library of Medicine (NLM) and National Institutes of Health (NIH) provide this resource for the benefit of clinical studies and participants, the information itself comes from each study's sponsor or principal investigator. It hasn't been reviewed by the government or approved by the Federal Drug Administration (FDA).

"ClinicalTrials.gov is a database of clinical trials and studies to help people potentially find innovative treatments for diseases," Nicole continues. The site serves scientists, physicians, and patients alike—and with those different audiences come different expectations, levels of expertise, scientific savvy, and health literacy. Those factors combine into especially sensitive and mission-critical communication.

"One of the challenges for the National Library of Medicine is technicality in language. A medical or legal professional may want to use words that are accurate and precise, but they're not the words the public relates to," she explains. "The language on the site was true in one way, but wasn't getting through to readers because it didn't mean anything to them. People didn't understand what they were getting into."

What people were getting into could present far greater
risk—with far less government oversight—than they anticipated. In June 2015, three patients separately sought an
experimental treatment for age-related macular degeneration (AMD), the leading cause of vision loss in people over 75
in the US. AMD is frustrating. There's currently no cure, but
treatments such as laser therapy or medication can slow the
progression of the disease. A study listed on ClinicalTrials.gov
promised hope in the form of stem cell injections, cultivated
from the patient's own fat and injected into each of their eyes.[3]
However the results of the trials, published two years after the
2015 listing, were far from hopeful.

"One-year outcomes are dramatically worse than the typical one-year visual-loss outcomes," reads an account in the
New England Journal of Medicine. "Although numerous stem-
cell therapies for medical disorders are being investigated at
research institutions with appropriate regulatory oversight,
many stem-cell clinics are treating patients with little oversight and with no proof of efficacy."[4] Rather than saving or
restoring their eyesight, the injections led to hemorrhaging
and retinal detachment for all three patients who sought treatment through the study they had found on ClinicalTrials.gov.

"At least one of the patients thought the procedure was
performed within the context of a clinical trial. However, the
consent forms signed by all three patients do not mention
a clinical trial. The patients paid for a procedure that had
never been studied in a clinical trial, lacked sufficient safety
data, and was performed in both eyes on the same day. Experimental bilateral intravitreal injections are both atypical and
unsafe," the report concludes.

How did these patients arrive at such an unfortunate and unintended outcome? They put undue faith and wishful belief in the safety of medicine simply because it was made available through a government site. They didn't always understand the risks associated with procedures or review them with familiar medical practitioners—even though statements on the site recommended that step. "If it's a dot-gov domain, people feel like it's official and someone must have reviewed and approved the content," Nicole says. But content is only as good as the people and processes behind it. Ironically, government content often lacks governance, especially if departments are underfunded and lack dedicated writers, designers, and editors. To help make up the difference, clear messaging, warnings, disclaimers, and open dialogue can span some of the gap—but only if it's accessible to the audience. If the viewer doesn't get it, you've failed to communicate. With impenetrable disclaimers and long walls of text, ClinicalTrials.gov failed its audience in a spectacular fashion.

"Good content is a conversation, and you need to have conversations with the people you're going to serve," Nicole explains. "But even though there was a big disclaimer on the site, people weren't reading it because it wasn't written in plain language." Trial participants weren't acting out of informed, educated trust. Instead, they acted on faith, sidestepping the process of empowerment through self-education.

"Let's say you have diabetes, or PTSD. If you're talking to a researcher or medical advisor and they're discussing trial options with you, they'd say, 'I want you to know, some of the trials I'm going to show you aren't reviewed by the government.' You'd want to talk about the risks and benefits with your doctor. Imagine the in-person interaction if you sat down with someone: they wouldn't read 12 paragraphs of legalese to you. They'd say, 'Hey, you should know this before you get started.'" Nicole is describing the differences between written and oral warnings, but also the difference between formal, comprehensively detailed disclaimers and the kind of consultative, back-and-forth conversations that meet patients' most pressing concerns and add in details along the way.

While chatbots might offer a way to triage just-in-time warnings, as of this writing they don't offer the structure, specificity, and nuance suitable for this context. ClinicalTrials.gov embraced a more fundamental approach suitable to any organization that needs to balance technical or cautionary information with the goal of helping users read, consider, and act: they get conversational and break up the text.

Consider the old approach of long paragraphs. They're visually monotone, with little typographic hierarchy to support the kind of scanning that allows readers to find the information that's not just important, but specifically important *to them* in the moment—i.e., relevant. Long paragraphs don't help users help themselves; they're not empowering.

"Small, manageable chunks of information are easiest for people to digest," offers Nicole. Chunked content also gives each concept the space and time to stand on its own, relevant to distinct contexts. "Legal teams don't always believe in progressive disclosure, but it's more realistic to give people information at the moment they need it." In that way, each concept gets the time and attention it deserves—in the context where it's relevant and makes the most sense. "If someone hasn't even found a trial, you don't want to hit them with 20 different caveats for a specific trial yet," she adds. "You don't want to hit them with a wall of text," especially if they're still building confidence in the topic and their own comfort with the idea of participating in a clinical trial. That kind of situation is more suited to a back-and-forth conversation. Conversation uses slang, incomplete sentences, and colloquial phrasing to build rapport and comfort—and so does Clinical-Trials.gov. "We use words you'd want to use while talking to them, rather than putting precision over clarity." That shift—putting clarity over precision—helps make the site and its disclaimers more accessible to more people.

"We used to say, 'Before participating in this study, talk to your medical advisor,' but 'medical advisor' sounds clumsy," Nicole continues. "Ads say, 'Talk to your doctor before trying Viagra,'" but that phrasing may leave out some people, such as patients who see a nurse practitioner. "'Medical advisor' represents a broader group of advocates, but then we're asking the reader to wonder who that is, and we're shifting the cognitive load onto them." Nicole notes that site visitors may already be reading—or skipping—the content in an anxious state of heightened emotion. While "medical advisor" is accurate, if people don't read it or understand it, it doesn't work. Today, the site offers a happy medium. It says, "Talk to your healthcare provider" to cover a broader range of practitioners with a term more people understand.

Unpack technical concepts
to make knowledge more inclusive

You'll also see efforts to eliminate extraneous details, avoid specialized terminology, and navigate emotionally fraught subjects in the digital service standards of the British National Health Service. The NHS website supports more than 40 million page views a month from people who are learning more about treatment for illness, medical advice, and general self-care. The service standard sets a high bar to meet the needs of all users in a diverse Britain, including "people with different physical, mental health, social, cultural, or learning needs."[5] User confidence grows by meeting people where they are. The NHS website works to educate users about personally relevant health topics and increases digital literacy to build their confidence and capacity for self-care. But it's not just people with a learning disability or with limited language skills who start at a deficit. The stress of sickness or a loved one's recent diagnosis can also make reading and research more challenging. Inclusive, accessible content and clear, navigable design makes information more useful and usable for anyone. With education comes empowerment, comfort, and trust.

"People who have poor health literacy tend to have poor health," explained Sara Wilcox, content designer for the NHS website in the UK, in an interview for the BBC.[6] At scale, the opposite can also be true: an investment in health education can counter poor health literacy and is an investment in public health. Health literacy refers to someone's ability to understand and apply information to make decisions about their own health. It offers quantifiable social and financial benefits for society, as well as more longterm benefits for nurturing individual confidence and maintaining trust in the much-loved NHS.

What does that investment in health literacy actually look like? It takes shape in the hard work of editing copy, translating jargon, and revising diagrams to remove details that obscure important takeaways. The first draft of communication can often force readers to work too hard to extract relevant meaning—at a time when they're least emotionally able to do that work. That's where editors, writers, and information designers can help. Think of easing the cognitive load for your users by chipping away at the words to make concepts clearer. You do the work of sculptors: carve away the rock until the inner form stands out.

"Healthcare journeys can be complex," notes the NHS Service Manual.[7] "Do the hard work to make things simpler." That statement may seem contrary to contemporary trends in content marketing, which recommend publishing more frequently and providing more curated content. With so many sites offering information aggregated from other sources, curation and creation can seem to be one and the same. Sites that offer the most pictures or blog posts are often rewarded with the top ranking in search results. But curators add value not by gathering, but by selecting: a commitment to quality and a singular perspective is what sets authoritative resources apart from content farms.

In textual content, that work looks like trimming down long, dense copy to only the most salient and relevant parts so as to not overwhelm a patient, then adding footnotes or pop-up commentary or definitions for those who want more detail. This approach applies to visual information as well. Whether you're a journalist publishing a photo gallery of a protest or the NHS sharing images to help patients understand when a skin lesion merits a visit to the dermatologist, more images aren't always better. Moreover, not all information is best communicated by images. The wrong images, or too many images, can confuse, overwhelm, and distract the viewer, whose primary goal isn't seeing images but using the knowledge they gain from them.

"Technology has made people sloppy," shared photojournalist Yunghi Kim in *Popular Photography*.[8] "Publications put up 60 images, but editing is part of the art form." It is stewardship of the user's experience, work that takes time and demands that the curator has a perspective on the topic. By advancing a calm, authoritative perspective and implicitly telling the viewer what's most relevant to their needs, the NHS helps people focus, learn, and move on with knowledge and confidence.

User feedback generally deems the NHS website as authoritative and trustworthy. In its commitment to be inclusive and accessible, the site leans into a tradeoff between the technical language of medicine and the vernacular language of people who come to the site for advice. Medical terminology may garner respect, but it's at the cost of clarity for the site's primary audience: patients. The Constitution of the NHS declares: "The patient will be at the heart of everything the NHS does," and it will offer "comprehensive service, available to all."[9] That core principle guided its formation more than 70 years ago but is still manifest today in tactical considerations of tone, design, and overall communication.

The NHS adopts a visual language to help the website feel familiar and help people easily identify it as the NHS. Trust in the entity lends trust to the website. Within the site itself, designers follow a simple color palette to help people understand navigation and the urgency of different types of content. "We use yellow for warning callouts and red for urgent care cards," explains the design system style guide.

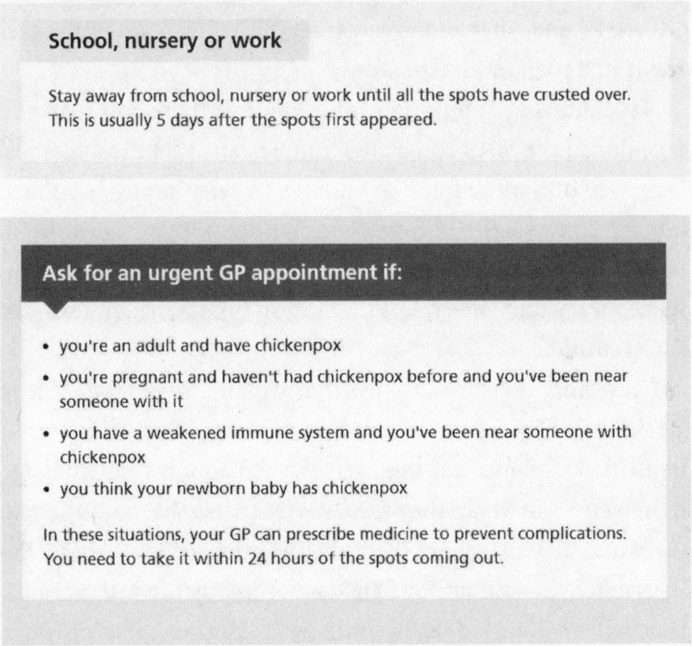

School, nursery or work

Stay away from school, nursery or work until all the spots have crusted over. This is usually 5 days after the spots first appeared.

Ask for an urgent GP appointment if:

- you're an adult and have chickenpox
- you're pregnant and haven't had chickenpox before and you've been near someone with it
- you have a weakened immune system and you've been near someone with chickenpox
- you think your newborn baby has chickenpox

In these situations, your GP can prescribe medicine to prevent complications. You need to take it within 24 hours of the spots coming out.

FIGURE 4.1 The NHS develops a consistent visual vocabulary: yellow— here, the lighter tone—advises, red prompts immediate action.

Typography also prioritizes familiarity and clarity. The site uses Frutiger, the typeface used by the NHS for more than 20 years—and by JFK International Airport in New York, Amsterdam Airport Schiphol, San Francisco's Bay Area Rapid Transit, and Warsaw's Zarząd Transportu Miejskiego transport authority. Contexts in which people often navigate under emotional stress are served well by familiar and clear typography. Adrian Frutiger designed the typeface to echo the proportions of Gill Sans, the typeface seen through much of GOV.UK, and offer the greatest legibility even when readers see it in a rush or at a distance.

In centering the patient and valuing their comfort and familiarity, the NHS translates complex and technical medical language into more familiar vernacular terminology and uses a more conversational tone. The site doesn't compromise on accuracy though. Clinicians review all information to confirm its accuracy and safety, but that doesn't mean it's unnecessarily scientific.

"'Pee' and 'poo'! Yes, that's what we use," says Sara Wilcox. The NHS website team researches and tests for the words that its British audience use themselves, then adopts that language to meet people where they are. "We try to use the words people use when they talk about their health and when they search the internet. We avoid jargon." Instead of "medicine interactions," they will spell out "does not mix with." Rather than "chronic," a term used by clinicians for extended duration but that many laypeople think means especially serious, they use "for a long time." In line with its core values, the NHS puts patients first. "We start with user needs," explained Sara on the NHS Digital blog. The content style guide goes into greater detail:[10]

We mostly use "poo", rather than "stool". We know that everyone can understand "poo", including people who find reading difficult.

We sometimes use the words "stool" or "bowel" when people will hear their GP use them. But we will explain the term or phrase. For example:

- "a sample of poo (stool sample)"

- "Bowel incontinence can affect people in different ways. You may have a problem if you have sudden urges to poo that you can't control."

While these familiar terms are accessible and clear, they're not without controversy. Some people complain that replacing urine and stool with pee and poo is simplistic or patronizing. But most users feel the language is direct and pitched at the right level. "Overall, we get more than 10 positive comments for every negative one," Sara reports. By starting with familiar vocabulary, an organization with specialized knowledge welcomes it audience to bring people into the conversation and increase their literacy—and confidence. The NHS website adopts a standard approach of prefacing more traditional phrases with familiar ones: "a sample of poo (stool sample)," for example. "That helps people learn the language of health," Sara explains.

Active voice also empowers the reader. "We use the active voice—'find a pharmacy' rather than 'a pharmacy can be found,'" explains the guide. That approach keeps the content and the reader focused on acting and advocating for themselves, a central tenet to modern partnership-oriented healthcare that promotes patients working in partnership with their health-care providers to maintain longterm health. The copy goes further, favoring a positive and personal tone, never beseeching or standing on ceremony. The content style guide breaks down key points of writing to build rapport and bolster the reader's confidence:

- Address the user as "you."

- Reassure by saying things like "Sertraline can cause side effects, but many people have no side effects or only minor ones."

- Empower by saying things like "talk to your doctor about..." rather than "your doctor will tell you about..."

- Avoid using "should" as it can sound patronising.

Combined with short sentences (no more than 20 words) and short paragraphs (no more than three sentences), the tone is direct, concise, and to the point. By rolling out a style guide with mandates for brevity *and* warmth, the NHS outlines a process to empower users through the written word.

Extend a hand to build confidence

As the NHS demonstrates, patient empowerment is vital to overall health and satisfaction in the system. Empowerment drives user satisfaction in any system, industry, or sector. If you can help your users feel more confident that they know what's going on—more confident in themselves—they'll be more confident in you too.

April Starr[11] discovered this firsthand when her husband, Lucas Daniel, was diagnosed with neuroendocrine cancer in 2017. He died only six weeks later. Both designers, they were used to jumping into unfamiliar industries and making sense of complex systems of information. Despite that background, their experience was marked by confusion, opaque communication, and despair. They wrestled with misleading jargon, unclear test results, and conflicting reports from multiple specialists. They didn't know how to make sense of the information they received to prioritize an action plan—until it was too late.

"In the end, I realized I was framing the problem wrong," April explains. "I was trying to get his cancer treated when I should have been focused on getting him a good death—and I wish I'd had more information so we could have made the switch sooner."

But framing the problem shouldn't have been the responsibility of the patient or his family. April didn't realize Lucas was going to die until the day before he died, when the palliative care team broke the news.

"Part of the experience Lucas and I had was that there were a lot of medical decisions to be made and we weren't given all the information to make informed decisions," she says. "We were dealing with cardiologists, kidney doctors, oncologists—and they were all giving conflicting information. Cardiology would say 'everything's looking great,' the kidney doctors would say 'let's get him on dialysis.' The palliative team finally said he was dying of cancer—so I was like, why are we doing dialysis?

"When we had to decide about moving forward with chemotherapy versus surgery, we didn't know about how the cancer had spread to multiple sites in his body. His oncologist never told us." April pauses. "I had received a remote second opinion through a service at Dana Farber and was reading through the report at the dinner table. At one point, it said 'I'm so sorry the cancer has spread to your skull,'" she recalls. The realization came as a shock, in part because it didn't fit in with their loose understanding of the situation.

"No one had explained to us the rate at which the cancer was growing. I felt like all my power was taken away. I started learning what I didn't know," she says.

What April and Lucas didn't know stemmed from their doctors' casual use of jargon, lack of coordination and prioritization within the team, and the couple's lack of knowledge about the impact of their decisions. They had to take it on themselves to get up to speed on the terminology.

"We needed help putting our personal data in context," she explains. "Like what's your cancer grade—and what's the definition of a cancer grade? Lucas's kind of cancer is always considered stage 4, but in other cancers, stage 4 is a death sentence." The confusion patients have around cancer grades mirrors the confusion the NHS discovered with clinicians' use of "chronic" and "acute" to describe longevity rather than severity, as laypeople tend to use the terms. "We also struggled to get useful answers because some test results seemed positive and others were negative, but there was no one doctor who coordinated what it all meant. Rather than results, we needed to see how it affected our decisions," she recalls. April and Lucas needed to know what the doctors knew about the impact of specific blood and chemistry markers on the big picture.

After Lucas's death, April designed the Cancer Worksheets, a set of straightforward charts that facilitate and capture the conversations and big picture of a patient's diagnosis and progress. They're not designed to be used on a screen or in an app. Instead, the patient or family members can print them and fill them out while huddling shoulder-to-shoulder with their doctors. They simplify complexity and encourage doctor-patient partnership.

"When you're first diagnosed, you need to know the basics," April explains. "Where is the cancer in your body? What is the treatment plan? What medications do we need to track? What symptoms do we need to track? We also need to track diagnostic test results. You want to compare them over time, and they're not always formatted so you can do that."

April's Cancer Worksheets help people feel more knowledgeable and confident that they know what's going on with their own care. That self-confidence reduces stress, and allows patients to feel more confident in the team of doctors supporting them. The worksheets may even help coordinate care so the team is more synchronized around the patient's needs rather than focused on competing areas of specialty expertise.

"I don't expect to understand health information and make all the decisions, but I expect to be a part of them," April concludes. "We didn't have medical knowledge, but we had an understanding of our lifestyle and quality of life and how we wanted to live. We should have had a say. But without the facts, how could we participate? With the worksheets, I hope to show that all you need to do is write this information on a piece of paper so someone feels like they have the

basic information and can participate in decision making."
By empowering patients with more information, the Cancer
Worksheets offer greater control over decisions of life and death.

An investment in plain language means trading impenetrable and unnecessary complexity for clarity. Calcified
language preserves our ivory towers; plain language flings
open their doors. If you want customers, users, and citizens
to be smart about helping themselves, you need to communicate in a way that lets them in. Do the work that demonstrates
care and respect: you respect your users most when you take
on the burden of making things clear and accessible for them.

By bringing tactical communication in line with that original vision, the NHS offers British citizens consistency that
inspires confidence and helps them become more active
participants in their own care. The work aligns with the mission of accessible service promised to the public more than
70 years ago. Savvy, active, engaged, educated, empowered,
confident—and more able to trust their own knowledge and
the advice of doctors and the medical system. Participants in
ClinicalTrials.gov enjoy the same benefits. Like the delivery
of modern medicine, this approach to communication isn't
easy. You'll need to put yourself not just in the situation of
the patient, but in their mind too. Draw on user research that
reveals what they need to know along the customer or patient
journey, as well as how they feel. Are you offering the right
information, and enough information, to clarify their choices
and feed their sense of self confidence?

Experts in many industries have long spoken with certainty and confidence. Now you face the opportunity to foster
some of that confidence in your audience. In medicine, public

health, email marketing, adult toys, apparel, and beyond, there's not one industry where the audience doesn't want to feel more confident about their knowledge and ability to make good decisions. Information delivered with clarity can strengthen that confidence. By building a consistent, humble, and clear voice, your brand earns trust by teaching people to trust themselves.

(II)

Volume

AS YOUR organization earns confidence by speaking clearly and consistently, you'll encounter a new question: how much should you say, anyhow? That's volume. Volume refers to how much you say, in length or level of detail. Longform content is in vogue, but it's not a license to babble or bottleneck more transactional experiences. Level of detail refers to visual content as well: the analog to longform copy is intricate imagery and enormous image galleries. But just as pithy quotations earn repetition, images that quickly convey concepts still earn the most attention and sharing. Memes are a testament to the speed of simplicity. Bullets and brevity still rule in corners of the online experience. Between long and short, detailed and abstract, we need to ask a more nuanced question: how much is enough?

A proposal, pitch, or statement of work is complete when it motivates a prospective client to sign off and approve it. It's a document optimized for action: complete with the right information and right level of detail, it helps the recipient feel confident in the approach—and confident in their own knowledge. Confidence is a sign of trust. A proposal or any kind of persuasive content is complete if it has enough information to empower a decision. If you want to quantify trust, count the decisions your content facilitates. Every signed contract is a testament to optimism, belief, and good faith.

Whether you're tasked with writing a blog post or aim to publish a report on the state of the industry, how do you know when you've said enough? How do you know when there are enough images in the gallery for an event? How do you know if you have the right images on a product description page to show the appropriate level of detail? And how do you know if you're showing or saying enough to help the prospect relate to the examples or imagery anyhow?

"Enough" is no absolute. Rather, "enough" is a variable that reflects the needs of an audience, their education and experience, and the stakes at play. High-risk, expensive decisions deserve more supporting information. For example, if you're in the market for a car, you probably want to know how it handles when you drive it. Perhaps you want to know what to expect for fuel economy. And if you care about how it looks, it's not enough to merely know that it's green. A few more adjectives or pictures are all the difference between getting a car in British racing green or an anemic 1970s seafoam.

But when is it too much information? For users who are trying to make quick decisions without fear of regret, detailed copy and visual richness only slows them down. If it doesn't speak to their needs, it's irrelevant. Respecting users' time and how much a brand or purchase matters—how much their choices matter—means offering enough content, but no more.

The right amount of content for a user to make a confident decision varies for audience, context, and industry—but there are many ways you can measure success. In some cases, you might want to decrease time on site if it's an indicator that people are able to get what they want and move on efficiently. The NHS aims to do that with pages that prioritize summaries to help people evaluate their symptoms quickly and decide if they need to seek further treatment. In other cases, you might define success by how long you can keep people immersed in content, such as an online community or experience supported by merchandising. If safari-era Banana Republic launched online today, they might adopt that definition of success to support confident decisions about premium-priced apparel or travel planning.

Streamlined visual content is a key element driving Apple brick-and-mortar stores to earn the most dollars per square foot of any retailer. Ads, promotions, and product fact sheets don't clutter the sleek, minimalist product displays and waiting areas, nor do visually stimulating patterns. At $5,500 in sales per square foot, Apple boasts more than five times the sales per square foot of Best Buy,[1] though Best Buy's price points are more diverse. Apple drives more successful sales by offering enough content to empower customers, but not so much as to distract them.

Less content isn't always right for every audience and business goal. At outdoor retailer Patagonia, expensive down jackets are detailed in long paragraphs and garden-path sentences. Lengthy bullet lists allow for side-by-side feature comparisons. Patagonia knows that more is more when it comes to creating confident customers. While the brand's website offers free shipping and free returns, Patagonia wants customers to make well-informed decisions so they don't buy something only to return it later. Those returns have a big carbon footprint—an important consideration for a company that aims to be carbon neutral by 2025.[2] Patagonia can measure "enough" content in part by a low return rate. It signals consumer confidence in their purchases and the products themselves. Those happy, confident customers also offer something beyond initial sales: loyalty and trust.

Earn trust by offering the people who use your content the right volume of information to feel knowledgeable and confident about their decisions. Whether your content is long and detailed or short and concise, the decision and the presentation is the result of hard work—work that you do so your user doesn't have to. In some cases, that work looks like first-person bench research, in the lab or the kitchen, and photos from behind the scenes that give credit to the man in the arena. In other cases, it looks like auditing and editing to reduce complex topics to simple, authoritative answers. We frame this work with examples to help our users relate to their own experiences—because by gaining knowledge and learning to trust themselves, they'll trust us too.

CHAPTER 5

Share your work
and remove all doubt

BRANDS EARN trust when they demonstrate authority and
expertise. But it's not enough to be the smartest brand in the
space or the smartest person in the room. You also earn loyalty by sharing that expertise, building the knowledge of your
customers and fans, and empowering the people around you
to make more confident decisions. Sharing takes time because
it's an investment in both doing the work and in documenting
it so your audience understands the details enough to trust
the process, even if they don't want to replicate the research
themselves. By exposing methodology, sharing experience,
and revealing detailed steps in an experience, your brand
also demonstrates respect for the reader and the time they
may need to weigh options and get comfortable with a decision. That's not an act of altruism; it's an investment in the
cycles of validation and deliberation that drive more confident
votes, purchases, and satisfaction. If you're the smartest person in the room, educate your audience so that they can see
and appreciate your value.

Do the work so your audience doesn't have to

Fans of America's Test Kitchen and its flagship magazine, *Cook's Illustrated*, know the media empire publishes content that isn't for the faint of heart. Its periodicals, much like its cookbooks, web properties, and television programming, promise nuanced explanations, thorough background notes, and thoughtful product comparisons. Complementing the copy are equally intricate illustrations and photographs that invite readers to carefully examine techniques and pore over details. In short, there are no breezy blurbs between these covers. More shiny cooking magazines support superficial scanning, but the editorial process at America's Test Kitchen goes beyond superficial in a test of time, objectivity, and painstaking detail.

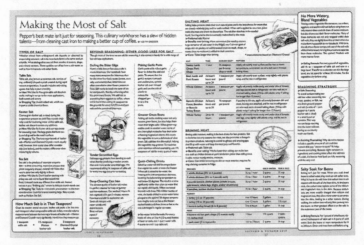

FIGURE 5.1 In *Cook's Illustrated*, rigor and attention to detail come through in extensive content about even the most otherwise overlooked topics.

That investment pays off threefold: readers trust the brand, put faith in the process, and gain something more personal. In a gestalt-like alchemy of trust and faith, home cooks build confidence in their own skills and savvy in the kitchen—all because of the exhaustive work of the team at America's Test Kitchen to "go there" and take risks so their readers don't have to.

To create each recipe, the team and their broader network of testers engage in extensive iteration and assessment of every variable. While you might know a few versions of a favorite cookie recipe, it can be intimidating to try a new ingredient or technique that breaks with tradition. Even if you're curious, the demands of a bake sale, holiday cookie exchange, or salivating family members often limit opportunities for experimentation and impose boundaries on personal experience.

The average recipe developed by America's Test Kitchen goes through 30 tests and eight test cooks who represent different specialties, preferences, and areas of expertise.[1] Equipment recommendations endure the same rigor. For an article presenting the best food processors,[2] the team put eight different models through more than 20 tests each to analyze the machines and develop solid recommendations to fit performance, pricing, and other needs of the audience. To evaluate and recommend the best 12-inch cast-iron skillet, for example, they seared, browned, and cleaned the top 10 through nearly a dozen different trials. Reading the recipe and process in "Best Ground Beef Chili,"[3] it seems natural to believe that the superlative title isn't so much a rave review but a statement of conclusive fact.

The scientific process practiced at America's Test Kitchen drives that belief. By openly laying out their steps, explaining how they guard against influence or subjectivity, and couching their methods in a matter-of-fact tone, the test cooks—writers themselves—don't demand leaps of faith. Instead, voluminous detail earns their readers' faith naturally as a byproduct of their process: the cooks start each recipe or equipment recommendation with many versions, then lay out the web of variables and take the time for excursions into special techniques or preparations that may demand additional explanation, whether in sidebars, illustrations, or specialist interviews. For example, in an evaluation of chef's knives, America's Test Kitchen sat down with a materials science professor at the MIT blacksmithing forge to better understand carbon steel. To explain the process of fermentation in bread-making, the team spoke with a microbial biologist. Beyond providing fascinating information, these conversations serve to further bolster the brand. America's Test Kitchen has earned a reputation for dependable results and trustworthy recommendations by revealing its cooks' methods, mistakes, and pitfalls, but its original research also fosters faith in the rigor of its process.

Beyond demonstrating rigor, those nuanced descriptions let even the most skeptical and demanding readers off the hook; they can feel confident in outcomes without having to do the research themselves.

Offer enough detail to engage every level of expertise

The rigor at America's Test Kitchen is a key difference from brands that bulk up content to achieve volume without value, or brands that demand respect without proof. Where so many chefs and cookbooks trade in pretense and intimidation by name-dropping rare ingredients or French phrases, *Cook's Illustrated* inundates readers with its process instead. Rather than spotlighting a single touted recipe of a celebrity chef, America's Test Kitchen teems with the benchwork of a crew working tirelessly to find the merits of their subject matter.

"Our editorial model is founded on the idea of collaboration," explains Jack Bishop, chief creative officer of America's Test Kitchen. "I think of Julia Child as the classic model of recipe development. She offered the experience of an individual expressed in recipe development—but that's not what we're doing here. It's not about an individual's vision, but about the scientific method. It provides us a solid framework. The method is what surfaces, not the ego."

And rather than publish in service to a celebrity chef, America's Test Kitchen serves someone else: the home cook. It's you—the reader, the viewer, the person putting dinner on the table tonight—who they labor to honor through their methodical process and detailed guidance.

"People say our recipes are long, and yes, sometimes they have a lot of steps," Jack admits. "But sometimes it's because we're providing so much description! We want to make sure you fully intend to do what you need to do!" He speaks with the same energy and precision for which America's Test Kitchen itself is famous. "The history of recipes builds from notecards that were like a shorthand; they assumed you spoke the same language, like more of a memory aid. There was no 'here's how you do this.' But here, we're going to give you that detail. We'll say what you can substitute. We need to write so it works for everyone."

To ensure recipes work for everyone, America's Test Kitchen invests in supporting a diverse audience: it includes novice cooks, skilled home chefs, people baking at different altitudes, and people with varied access to ingredients, cultural touchstones, and physical needs. Those requirements influence the range of products and equipment recommendations: nothing can be arcane or impossible to find, or accessible only to cooks in major metropolitan areas. Those requirements also influence the diversity of their testers, who include tall people stooping over the counters and shorter people angling to pour from heavy mixing bowls. Perhaps most visibly, audience awareness also drives the level of detail in visual and verbal explanations.

Jargon also affects the volume of detail a brand uses in communication. Economical catchphrases and acronyms can save time and build rapport by subtly delineating an in-crowd, but they do little to educate the broader audience and build the audience over time. "We try to use as little jargon and technical language as possible," Jack cautions, in an industry where even everyday cooking techniques are often obscured by the nomenclature of scientific processes—or assumptions of oven calibration. "We never say 'bake for 30 minutes' but instead 'bake until it looks like this, feels like this; and that's *about* 30 minutes.' The reality is our ovens are never perfectly calibrated, but we can all have good results if we know what the end product should look like, smell like, and even sound like." Those details demand writers' time and attention, especially in an age when not everyone is familiar with the smell of bread fresh from the oven, and even fewer people remember seeing parents or grandparents thump the bottom of a loaf to listen for that low, hollow sound echo through warm caverns of air.

Facilitate success to breed confidence, regardless of platform

"We teach people to use all their senses when they're cooking, not just robotically follow the recipe, because success breeds confidence," Jack says. *Success breeds confidence.* More so than any motivational speaker, the test cooks are in the business of empowerment. Amid paragraphs about the sound of bread and the smell of sauce, confidence is the real product of America's Test Kitchen. Readers learn to check in with their own senses, and trust themselves just as much as they trust the recipes.

"People say the main obstacle to cooking is time," he continues. "I don't believe it. The main obstacle is failure. People decide to start cooking and fail, and it reinforces the feeling they can't cook. But this isn't rocket science. Everyone is capable of cooking. When you start to succeed, following the recipe, you develop confidence. And sometimes get to the point where you don't always need the recipe."

Readers' time may have little impact on their enthusiasm for cooking, but that's in large part thanks to how America's Test Kitchen spends its time. Test cooks hone content throughout the editorial process and restructure it for different platforms. In short, they do the work so readers don't have to. Regardless of the platform on which their audience encounters a recipe, they can depend on the content benefitting from the strengths of that platform. For example, a home cook might first learn about Millionaire's Shortbread

on the *America's Test Kitchen* television show. Its gooey caramel comes under the spotlight on season 18 in an episode
titled "Elegant Desserts." Fans of the recipe eager to bring the
flavor home—shortbread never had it so good, draped under
inexplicably satisfying chocolate and caramel—don't need to
record the episode though. They can sit back and enjoy the
repartee and play-by-play, then pull out the November 2016
issue of *Cook's Illustrated* to reference the article and recipe
in full.[4] The conversation among the chefs makes for great
TV, in the many-to-one style of broadcast communication,
but that platform doesn't work well for conveying detailed
instructions. Instead, the methods can gain the attention they
deserve in the more intimate reading experience of a magazine. Social media offers value at the other extreme: they can
whet the appetites of readers with brief glimpses of recipes
in development that don't yet have the production value of a
stylized magazine shoot.[5]

America's Test Kitchen "breaks the fourth wall" to speak
directly to the audience and use a more action-oriented style
of photography to bring viewers into the process and behind
the scenes—notes, spills, and all.

"No one wants a 30-minute story on making a croissant
on Instagram," Jack explains. "But if we're testing coolers
and sawing them in half? That's perfect for Instagram. It's
fun for that platform. We work to create the right content
for every platform." America's Test Kitchen also focuses on
translating its stories to take advantage of each platform
or device's unique strengths. This approach fits into their
broader embrace of adaptive content: they tailor the delivery

America's Test Kitchen ✔
@TestKitchen
Following ⌄

#BehindTheScenes #Snapshot **Million Dollar Shortbread** ift.tt/1S632gv

9:06 AM - 17 Mar 2016

FIGURE 5.2 Tweets from America's Test Kitchen welcome fans into the kitchen without the polish of a professional photoshoot or the thoughtful detail of photography in *Cook's Illustrated*.

of information to address the user's context and optimize content types for specific use cases.

Consider a single subject, such as the recipe for the best beef chili. On social media, 10-second video snippets attract readers to 20-minute real-time cooking videos. The November 2015 issue of *Cook's Illustrated* offered the recipe over a few pages, complete with photographs to compare different cuts of meat and demonstrate the browning process. This format is ideal for a reader who's eager to sit down and invest some time in the latest issue. Online, the recipe gains even more context: paragraph after paragraph offers the backstory, history, and wisdom from research that tests hypotheses on optimizing the depth of flavor and tenderness of the meat. But what if you're trying to prepare the recipe, without extraneous commentary? If you're in your kitchen, you can grab your tablet or phone, swipe through the recipe as a slideshow, and see the content as stand-alone captions under photos that illustrate each step. Nothing is more important than the user's context—and context drives the delivery, format, and volume of content.

"The captions have everything you need to cook, right in the slideshow," Jack notes. "So it doesn't say just 'heat the oil,' but 'heat one tablespoon of olive oil.' We specify the type and amount right there in the caption because if you're cooking from an iPad, you don't want to keep scrolling back to the ingredient list." With success as a goal, the test cooks edit and translate content so readers can always work effectively with the medium and device they have at hand.

America's Test Kitchen uses a tone that isn't for everyone, but the time it invests in backstory is valuable for the type of cook who reads it—and the cooks who simply appreciate knowing it's there for reference. They may not care to replicate the research but take comfort in knowing if they wanted to, they could. Prefacing each recipe is a section titled "Why This Recipe Works." It recalls the familiar challenges people encounter while making other versions of the recipe—maybe how the dark meat and white meat never cook at the same rate, or how the flavor of the common chocolate chip cookie always lacks depth. Then it shares how the new and improved version is more satisfying. (Spoiler: brown the butter in your chocolate chip cookies to balance the sweetness and bring out a nutty flavor.)

While teachable moments in the sidebars and spotlights on specific techniques aren't required reading, they support different types of readers. "Our readers are trying to build their skills," Jack says. Unlike cooks who follow a specific chef or seek inspiration for a culinary vacation, home cooks value America's Test Kitchen for that learning experience—and the shared understanding of those goals. "They view cooking as an avocation, not just a chore that has to be done. They're on a journey where they're learning, so we take tangents and step back to inform what they're doing," he explains. Education begets success, and success engenders empowerment and increased confidence. Across channels and mediums, that process repeats in kitchen after kitchen: education fuels empowerment, and their faith in the research process translates to trust in the brand and confidence in themselves.

Be the first person in first-person research

It's not only cooks who enjoy combing through details, product comparisons, and explanatory illustrations as they build their knowledge and confidence. Since 1974, audiophiles, hobby photographers, and AV nerds have gained a similar sense of trust in Crutchfield, the online electronics retailer. Crutchfield's fans invest time reading about home and car audio equipment, camera gear, home theater installations, and other electronics. Crutchfield's extensive collection of videos, infographics, and product descriptions created by sales associates helps them support that kind of ongoing education.

"I'm a big believer in longform copy and helping people get as much information as they can or want," explains Steve Kindig, senior home audio video editor at Crutchfield, where he's worked more than 30 years. "So many of our products are pretty complicated. It's not like buying a shirt or sofa. It takes a lot to explain to a person what's going on—or to show them that maybe a product won't meet their needs. Customers have commented that our salespeople will recommend a lower priced item than what they were considering. Our salespeople have so much product knowledge that they can usually ask just a couple of questions and zero in on what someone needs."

By coupling education with personal support, Crutchfield serves both people who need direct guidance and those who would rather be left alone to gather information at their own pace. Those people can scroll through seemingly endless pages that describe an associate's personal experiences installing a new stereo system or exploring the utility of a new camera lens. Their first-person accounts are illustrated with diagrams comparing user interfaces and photographs depicting workarounds, after-market tweaks, and other ideas that go beyond the manual. As customers gain product knowledge, they gain confidence in their own ability to make a savvy, informed decision—the right decision that won't be tainted by buyers' regret.

Whether they're eager for assistance and reassurance from a sales associate or more interested in immersing themselves in the research without interruption, both customer personas benefit from the way Crutchfield has evolved in its approach to content and customer education.

In 1975, Crutchfield reached out to customers to gather initial feedback on its product catalogue. This early user research transformed corporate communications. The catalogue relaunched less than six months later as a "magalogue" with more explanation, original research, and longform copy. Sales took off. Steve Kindig's career at Crutchfield mirrored the company's growth. He moved from customer engagement to content creation and let the former influence the latter with terrific results.

"When I first started, I began in catalogue requests. When folks called in, I wrote down their names and addresses. Then I moved into phone sales for a year," Steve says. "But a position opened to help write the catalogue—and I was the first person there who had been in phone sales. I'd been talking to a lot of customers and developing in-depth product knowledge." It was the mid-1980s and phone sales were similar to consultative, face-to-face engagement with salespeople in physical stores. "At the time, we had maybe 10 salespeople. On a typical day, they might talk to 100 people—so you had to develop knowledge pretty quickly," he says. Prospective customers were interested in stereo equipment but came to the conversation with existing knowledge as well as more challenging questions.

"The questions they'd ask sometimes weren't covered in the presentations we'd get from vendors," Steve explains. "So we'd need to dig further." They took measurements of products or took them apart. "When I started writing for the catalogue, an editor asked me to write down what to change. I gave him a long list, all based on what I'd heard from customers on the phone. My contribution to Crutchfield's content over the years has been to focus on being accurate and complete. In the web age, most online retailers just copy and paste the vendor descriptions on to their sites—but we've never done that. We came to be known as a very reliable source of information; there have been many times over the years where our information has been even more accurate than the vendor's," he notes. That's due in large part to the goals and perspective Crutchfield brings to its work. Rather than trying to sell its products, sales associates are merely trying to understand them. Much like the test cooks at America's Test Kitchen, Crutchfield's associates explore, compare, and test options, all for the benefit of their customers.

"Vendors' brochures are typically produced by their marketing departments," Steve explains. "But when we get in there, our product research team opens every box, takes the gear out, takes measurements. They get information from the horse's mouth, the owners' manual, the holy grail of accurate information—which may be different than the marketing materials we've been supplied. We learn how to hook things up and get that deep, hands-on experience. When vendors come in and do training, as soon as it's over, our people are up there, taking things apart—and even during, they're peppering the vendors with questions."

All that first-person research allows the Crutchfield team to stand in for its customers and do the kind of research they'd want to do—if the option to "try before you buy," test at home, and open up the inner workings of electronic equipment was available across all products, price points, and return policies.

Empirical research is meaningful: if we don't have access to experts or friends with similar needs and their own personal experiences, we look for opportunities to gain information and courage in our convictions through our direct observation. Retailers like Best Buy, a Crutchfield competitor, create this context by inviting customers into Magnolia Home Theaters in their brick-and-mortar stores. There, customers shopping for home audio can sit down in private demo rooms to examine and compare sound quality. Sales associates offer some product knowledge, but the experience is constrained by the products on hand, the expertise of particular associates, and the store environment itself.

But online, shoppers don't face those constraints, and Crutchfield pushes the opportunities afforded by the internet. In addition to original content on product pages, their website offers a section with more editorial content like buying guides, category introductions, product reviews, and personal trip log-style posts.

"I'll be talking about my thought processes and priorities for the room, and including plenty of details on the various construction stages, gear selection, and the final results," Steve wrote in a 2010 post titled "Transforming a Basement into a Home Theater."[6] With the tone and transparency of a friend, he levels with readers about his priorities, such as minimizing sound vibration and ensuring a room is big enough "so my audience wouldn't be required to crush together in one big armchair to watch a movie." By clarifying his goals, he helps readers put his recommendations in the context of their goals. Don't anticipate a crowd? No need to limit your walls to narrowly spaced beams. Don't plan on frequently swapping out components? Don't worry about optimizing for an AV cabinet with its own HVAC ducts.

The post doesn't shy away from details, supplementing the lengthy copy with photos of framing, the equipment closet layout, and optimal insulation for soundproofing between and along the studs and ceiling joists—and that's all before readers dig into the actual equipment recommendations. As with recipes in *Cook's Illustrated*, it offers detailed asides to weigh the pros and cons of specific techniques; here, readers can consider their own needs and build knowledge. One sidebar breaks down the topic of "equipment racks: free-standing versus built-in." Need to be neat? Go with built-in racks. Want to ensure long-lasting performance? Choose a free-standing rack to rest on your concrete floor where components are less likely to pick up vibrations.

Humanize the work

We research products or companies, but we *relate* to people. Humans trust humans. By speaking in the first person, you remind people of the humans behind the content and behind the brand. Crutchfield promotes a visual and verbal style that simulates first-person engagement. "We write in the first person where it makes sense," explains Steve. The writers embrace a conversational style that reveals warmth, humor, and humility. "I loved my phone camera, but it wasn't long before I started getting frustrated by its many limitations. It became clear that if I wanted to learn how to take better photos, I was going to need a better camera," begins Deia Zukowski, managing editor of home electronics learning content at Crutchfield, in "How to Choose the Best DSLR Camera for a Beginner,"[7] an article targeting customers considering their first camera with interchangeable lenses.

The human element is evident in more than just the writing. There are photos of a sales team in the parking lot installing a car stereo. The pictures show how associates remove trim panels, reroute wires, and navigate tricky mounting systems. Close-up imagery doesn't put the product on a pedestal. Instead, it includes their hands to put the effort in context. Articles, reviews, and customer service content are also often accompanied by headshots of advisors. "It's the people here who make us different. We promote our folks as helpful and knowledgeable. So often when you call a company, they're working from a script—but not our tech support," Steve notes. If the old adage is "products don't sell product, people sell product," Crutchfield is acutely aware and proud of its core differentiator and real product: advisors "sell" empowerment. Their customers buy confidence. Advisors can spend hours on the phone with individual customers to help them think through options in a purchase, navigate a complex installation, or troubleshoot technical problems. The products listed on the website are available from many retailers, but the combination of expertise, education, and empowerment is far more difficult to find.

This degree of customer service and original content is expensive. But it's an investment in the brand itself. Julie Govan, the brand manager at Crutchfield, describes the sentiment and strategy that drives this level of service.

"We want everyone to have enough confidence in the information they see to make them feel like they can make a decision—and feel good about it from the moment they click 'Add to Cart' until it arrives at their house. People who are not confident in what they're getting either won't buy or won't be happy with what they get. So it's really important for them to be the decision maker, not us," she explains.

Let learning take the time it takes

Many people are more comfortable offloading the effort, research, and responsibility of decisions about electronics to someone else—and often delegate complex choices to seemingly more knowledgeable salespeople. But that's not right for all brands or all customers. By surveying users and analyzing website analytics, Crutchfield has learned what's right for *its* customers. They're people who don't offload the research, but revel in it. They don't mind the time it takes. The customer contact center offers a window into their process.

"Some customers call or chat because they're close to purchasing and want to validate a specific thing before moving forward," Julie explains. These customers have spent a significant amount of time on the site, poring over articles and weighing their options. Longform copy, detailed imagery, and comparison tools give them the time and space to engage in cycles of deliberation and validation.

Those patterns may feel familiar. If you're shopping online and considering an expensive purchase, notice the time between putting an item in your shopping cart and checking out. On sites like outdoor apparel retailer Patagonia.com, a new jacket may cost a few hundred dollars. Rather than rush you through that purchase, Patagonia prompts you to consider and confirm the size and color you want, even with merchandise already in the shopping cart. Their approach is not unlike how shopkeepers have always engaged their customers in brick-and-mortar stores. In a convenience store, you can rush in and out and not spend more than 30 seconds considering what type of soda you want to buy. As the name implies, it's convenient. But if you're browsing in a boutique, the owner may approach you with product suggestions, offering a shirt that would work well with your bag or coloring. They don't want to rush you through a purchase. Online, principles of "slow content strategy" drive similar modes of interaction. Patagonia offers opportunities and additional content to help you consider the purchase, check in with your gut, and feel good about the money you're about to spend. Crutchfield's content and customer service interaction offers those same benefits.

Of course, not all shoppers are ready to buy. "We often have customers who contact us because they know what they want to achieve, or they want a certain kind of experience, but they don't know how to get it. They know what they want but need help navigating the details," Julie says. Whether a customer wants crisp sound quality, the ability to take photos in low light, or the ability to cancel ambient sound on a long flight, Crutchfield's contact center offers them a style and tone of support that helps them get smarter about their needs and options so they can make better and more confident decisions.

"Our contact center has been trained to figure out the customer's situation: what they need, how they're going to use it, who else is in the home. We figure that out, then when we have a good understanding, point them toward the thing that matches what they describe. We know the ins and outs of the product; but they know what's most relevant for them," says Julie. "If we have personal experience relevant to them, we'll share it, but we're not encouraged to sell certain things. No one gets penalized if a customer gets off the phone without buying—and we don't do a lot to get off the phone quickly."

Crutchfield also tries to meet the customer where they are. "We may be smart, but so is our customer," says Amy Lenert, Crutchfield's chief content officer. "We try to be sensitive to that fact; we don't want to force a solution." That respect might mean customers ultimately decide not to buy, or put off a purchase until they feel more comfortable with the decision, or decide to buy something at a lower price point per the advisor's guidance upon learning their goals.

"We listen and ask careful questions," Amy continues. "We're thoughtful. That mirrors the confidence we get from people." Crutchfield shares its customers' curiosity and confidence. Through education, it fosters empowerment. Mutual respect is a byproduct and vital component of that interaction. And as in any good relationship, respect is tantamount to trust.

CHAPTER 6

Say what you have to say, then stop

AMERICA'S TEST KITCHEN builds authority and gains trust by embracing the mantra of apron-clad grandmas everywhere who eye up their suspiciously skinny offspring: more is more. Crutchfield creates a similar kind of comfort through abundance. Across the pond in Great Britain, a different perspective, for a different topic and target audience, is finding equal success: brevity is the soul of wit—and can also drive confident action.

Skilled comedians know the value of a pause, in which what they don't say matters as much as what they do say. They let a punchline sink in to help an audience connect the dots in an anecdote, and come to the logical conclusion themselves, often in a way that's much more satisfying than if the person on stage had spelled out every detail. Brief, concise content can be just as powerful in the way it makes an audience feel smart and confident. It creates the space to let users consider what they've learned and respond appropriately; often, brevity is the restraint that fosters confidence and can prompt users to act.

British humor has a celebrated relationship with restraint, and now British government communication can stake a similar claim. GOV.UK presents information on UK public services, and it promises to do it in a way that is "simpler, clearer, faster." That tagline summarizes how the Government Digital Service consolidates information previously spread across 3,000 government websites in a single, authoritative, and complete site. But the site doesn't just present information as a public relations channel or communications vehicle. GOV.UK helps users find personalized information to register to vote, adapt to Brexit, renew a passport, apply for benefits, confirm statutory maternity leave schedules, and so much more. Its users demand accuracy and specificity because they won't (or can't) wade through an ocean of generalized statements to find what they need to know.

If that sounds like a lot, it is—but rather than serve up bulk to an individual user, the site thoughtfully triages and organizes content to meet their needs and interests. With expectations of detail, accuracy, and actionable information customized to each of the nearly 14 million people who visit the site each week, GOV.UK relies on a defined focus and efficient content design to be complete and offer the right amount of relevant content.

It's easy to think "enough" content is nothing short of extensive, but that was the old GOV.UK. Before a 2012 overhaul, the team published information about government services on some 75,000 pages, many of them outdated, contradictory, or byzantine. Users might have to read through multiple pages only to be referred to alternate sites, and still find only general, non-actionable information that referred them to in-person meetings. More content wasn't necessarily better content—and users knew it.

"Government was pumping out so much information people didn't know when they got to the end of it," reports Sarah Richards,[1] head of content design at the UK Government Digital Service (GDS). People often need a cue to stop gathering information and to start acting on it, a nudge that they should feel confident they have enough knowledge to submit a form, make a purchase, or cast a vote. Without a signal that they've reached the end or attained "enough," users end up in endless cycles of deliberation and validation. Analysis paralysis is familiar and unsettling. It's the anxiety of feeling never quite fully informed, then scrolling Twitter in hopes of catching up on the news, only to get lost in an endless stream. Or perhaps you've been caught in the Netflix abyss: on an unexpectedly empty Friday night, you find yourself so spoiled for choice that you continue to add to your queue, read reviews, and flit among two-minute trailers; in doing so, you delay an actual decision—and while away those rare hours until the only smart thing is to give up. Give up, go to sleep, and try again another day.

Giving up is exactly the response people had to previous versions of government services content. "To explain how to calculate your maternity pay, we'd had five 750-word articles," Sarah says. Content was framed by countdowns and anecdotes, such as articles like "Working When Pregnant."[2]

FIGURE 6.1 "Working When Pregnant," one of many articles on the UK government's former website that addressed maternity leave pay.

Moreover, the volume of information and various paths to take within the information were confusing—and frequently drove visitors to external resources.

"People would go to the BBC instead, because they trusted the BBC," she explains. Users turned to outside sources to get information on the government's official policy as well as services and processes when they couldn't be confident in the information they found on government sites—or when they just couldn't find the information at all.

Authoritative information was buried in other vaguely related content. The information that the government published (and then needed to maintain) included social perspectives, green living advice, and environmental science. Pages like "Keeping Bees" detailed the role of bees in the environment and how humans could help them by creating shelters, providing food, and limiting the use of pesticides by planting companion plants like marigolds near vegetables.

The content was interesting, but neither fully relevant to the work of government nor within scope for its oversight. As in any smart, purposeful content audit, the organization needed to first ask what was within their responsibility to do before they could determine what to cut.

Rein in scope

"Government should only do what only government can do" became a guiding mantra of the redesign, as documented in the Government Design Principles:[3]

1 Start with user needs.

2 Do less.

3 Design with data.

4 Do the hard work to make it simple.

5 Iterate. Then iterate again.

6 This is for everyone.

7 Understand context.

8 Build digital services, not websites.

9 Be consistent, not uniform.

10 Make things open: it makes things better.

This mandate helped GDS audit and cull content so they could prioritize what mattered. The content audit trimmed department sites from 75,000 pages down to 3,000. The pages about trends in beekeeping and other extraneous matters—all gone. Those topics were better addressed by organizations that offered comprehensive topical guidance, such as BeeBase.[4]

After cutting away content better served by organizations outside of government, GDS could take a more constructive approach to planning new content. Guiding this approach was their users—specifically, their users' needs. Many organizations, public and private, talk about user-centered design, but still start with the products and channels their clients seek: websites, new social media campaigns, or day-long conferences. The GDS perspective of following users' needs is different from delivering websites, producing infographics to an editorial calendar, or publishing blog posts to maintain visibility. Those content marketing efforts can be an outcome of content strategy, but cannot replace a need-driven content strategy.

What can *only the government* do when it comes to working with bees? Though there are many sources of information about trends and best practices in beekeeping, only the government can publish the application for a license[5] to release non-native bumblebees for bee pollinator research initiatives. *Only the government* can provide health certificates to import bumblebees from EU member states to the UK—and advise how to prepare your business for the impact of Brexit and its transition period in regard to the import of animals, livestock, and insects.

Meeting those needs and answering questions fundamental to users' business and personal lives drives the scope of content. In any organization, communication can reflect a brand-driven content strategy by prioritizing the qualities a business wants to own in the hearts and minds of its target audience. Qualities like *simple, streamlined, innovative,* and *anticipatory* come through in GOV.UK's white space and in the flat areas of color that frame the copy. They continue through concise introductory copy that asks direct questions and offers short, declarative page summaries. If this brand-driven content strategy informs how the content sounds and looks, user needs inform what the content addresses—with a healthy dose of empathy and humility.

"Government needs to give users information they need so they can control their situation or take control of what's going on," Sarah explains. "Nobody wants to go to government. No one browses government sites. You're either giving money, getting money because you don't have enough, or doing something to keep out of jail—so you want to do it as quickly as possible and get out."

The notion that nobody wants to browse your site can be a harsh reality for copywriters and designers that serve more transactional organizations. People likely don't visit for long yarns or to feed their feature curiosity. People come to meet specific needs, needs that are but one part of a larger context. If you're a product owner, founder, marketer in a mission-driven organization, or copywriter who's been hearing daily buzz from the engineering team, you probably thrill at sharing the good stories that jostle to get out of your organization. It's tempting to start every product demo or web page by focusing on the latest features—or the organization's mission statement, or celebrated history. But think about what your brand needs to communicate in the context of what your audience needs to learn. Our sites matter less than we think—but the information they offer is of critical importance in the moment people need it.

GDS balances empathy to its users' goals with the humility of understanding the value of content in larger contexts by prioritizing user needs. "Start with user needs," is the first article in the Government Design Principles. Of course, if you're a writer who's been privy to the features planned for each release, it's tempting to start the conversation there. Or if the creative brief calls for a sweeping pan shot of the shiny new product, it's easy to start dreaming about the dramatic lighting. But smart content design can help reset the strategy. Users don't shop for features, or fables. They shop for benefits first, then features. *What's in it for me?* Focus on users' needs, then you can help them focus on the features and details that will make a difference in their decisions.

If you're determining scope for an enormous initiative, it can be an unwieldy process. Maybe you don't confront work on a scale or budget like that of GOV.UK. On a smaller initiative, with tighter budget, fewer people, and limited timeline, there's even less room for wasted effort. It's even more important to clarify the scope. GDS prioritized their work by first determining user needs.

They looked to the former site's search logs and pages to reverse engineer a list of some 1,800 user needs, such as "I need to get a passport" or "I need to change the address on my vehicle registration." The team assigned each need a priority and a tracking number and entered it in a tool they dubbed The Needotron. There, they evaluated whether it would fit in the scope of the beta. Did search history indicate people wanted it? Was it reasonable to expect that it was something government should do—and was it something only government could do? Did it encourage a shift to digital service delivery? These questions helped to further narrow the scope by nearly half. The Needotron helped focus the team's efforts, attention, and budget on the task ahead: designing to help users more effectively meet their own needs through interaction with government.

Focus users' attention on what matters

After determining the scope and schedule of priorities for the beta, GDS gained clarity of purpose for content design. Now they needed to ensure that their users' engagement with the content maintained a similar focus. For example, consider the challenges of budgeting in a small business with uncertainty over Value-Added Tax (VAT). If a cafe owner needed to determine the taxes they would need to pay to import coffee,[6] they could easily grow frustrated with the details and data that obscured the information that was most important.

Variables around the product types, footnotes that demand additional attention, and assorted disclaimers undermine the user's confidence in the accuracy and completeness of information—and in the process itself.

The GOV.UK interim beta redesign[7] triaged and tiered information so users never have to choose among too many variables at once. Easier questions (roasted or not? decaf or not?) allow users to focus on one variable at a time, and help them build confidence in themselves that radiates into confidence for the system. By presenting the content in a tree structure, the design demands more clicks but reduces the

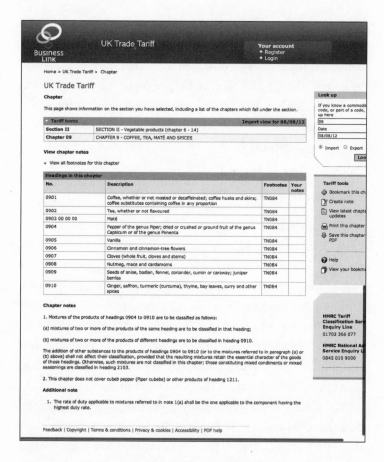

FIGURE 6.2 The trade tariff guidelines on the UK government's old website were too detailed to be usable or useful.

chance that users will miss a key variable along the way and make a mistake that requires they start over.

The subsequent and, as of this writing, final design release[8] of the trade tariff tool reflects similar methods for helping

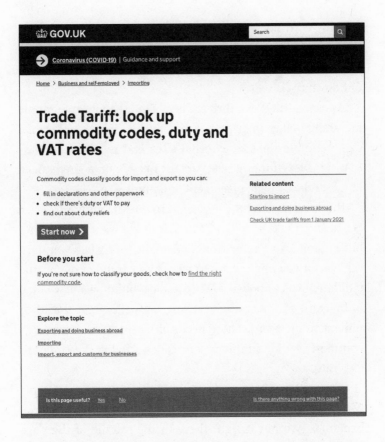

FIGURE 6.3 The trade tariff tool on the UK government's new website provides useful information in just a few steps.

users focus on their questions and build confidence through self-service.

Like the beta, it opens with copy that orients the user and tells them what to expect. The bold page title clarifies the three main things you can do through the tool. Additional opening copy helps the user scan visually for keywords that may reflect the needs they had in mind, like "duty reliefs." And a warning note explains what to expect regarding the known unknowns of Brexit.

As users drill down through layers in the tool, typographic hierarchy makes their path clear—as does what's *not* on the page: endless links to external sites and related footnotes. Instead, everything the user might need is on a single page, in hierarchy by page placement and point size.[9]

But how does GDS even begin to wrestle with a topic as broad and multifaceted as VAT? You might want to pay a VAT bill, submit a VAT return, or confirm the VAT when you sell a vehicle. Or you might want to report VAT fraud or determine if different rules apply if you're disabled, building a new home, or budgeting for a new advertising campaign for a charity or philanthropic event. Those needs are important—but not as common as a far simpler user need: verifying the standard VAT rate.

"Here, VAT is 20% and we know that 80% of the people with questions about VAT just want that number," Sarah explains. "We put it right there in the middle of the page because we narrowed [the purpose] down to the user task and so we take care of it in one place." If you need additional information, sidebar links lead you to related content on how to charge VAT and other taxes. Copy below the main area offers minimal detail on reduced rates and exemptions, in short, single-sentence paragraphs and a simple black-and-white table. For the users outside the 80%, the site meets their needs in an extensive, hierarchical section that supports them

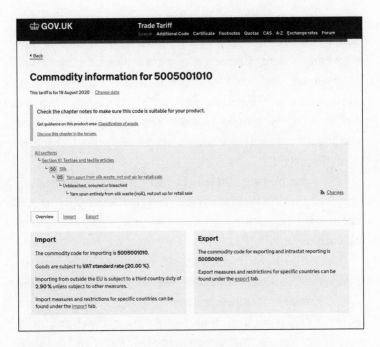

FIGURE 6.4 On one page, tariff seekers in the UK can now scan for and find everything they need to complete the task.

with detail—but for the core audience, those details don't clutter a page that aims to provide a quick answer.

For users who previously turned to the BBC or other sources to get quick and authoritative information, the page's design is minimal, and *enough*. Related information is available but out of sight, creating a calm sense of organization. As with America's Test Kitchen, GOV.UK fosters confidence by showing how additional information is available, even if users don't need it in the moment. The abundance is organized.

"Now you can see the edges of the content, so people know when they get to the end of a subject," Sarah describes. The edges are evident parameters of what topics are in the scope of discussion and what topics or pages are supplemental or unnecessary to helping people complete the task. "They can say 'oh, that's everything I need to know.' They become more confident because they know government's canonical source is on that page."

More complex content benefits from a similar essentialism and organization that helps GDS focus on the user needs and, in turn, help users focus on the most important information on each page.

The Child Benefit is a monthly allowance for caregivers that varies based on annual income. "Most people Google the benefit name and some variation of 'how to claim,' so that's how we decide on how to name the task and determine its edges," Sarah says. The section at the landing page[10] for child benefits details how to claim the benefit and how to change the claim or get additional help with it.

"It's not that we don't let you go beyond that, but that's as far as most people need to go," she notes. The sidebar links to adjacent topics: what to do when your child is no longer a minor, what to do in the event of a death, and calculators and calendars. They offer critically important information that's relevant to far fewer people. And users can gain this assurance by the content design of the page itself: the most space is dedicated to the core information necessary to receive the benefit, which also earns the biggest subheads and point size for body copy. The typography minimizes less essential content to instill a sense of confidence that it is whole and complete.

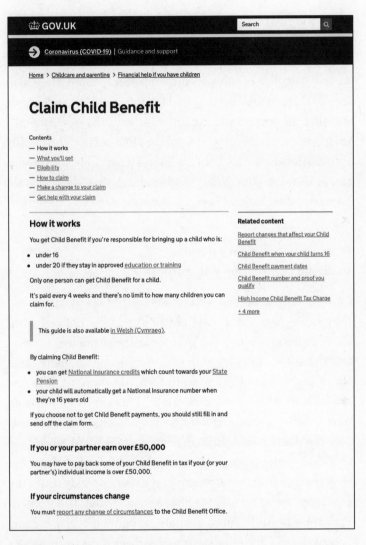

FIGURE 6.5 A single page on GOV.UK addresses the majority of needs for the majority of users interested in the topic.

"Previously, there was so much information about one topic that people couldn't trust it because they didn't know if they'd gotten to the end of it," Sarah explains. Just as people turned to the BBC for conclusive direction on a topic, they also looked there to feel like they had the full story. "Nine different websites all said something different with the government's information on one subject: from the Home Office, the Deputy Prime Minister, Ministry of Defence, Department for International Development. What we found was that people would go to the BBC instead because the BBC gave you the edges."

Remove unnecessary details to signal completion and authority

Copy that prefaces each section sets up the user to know what they can expect—and what not to expect. By delivering on those expectations in topic after topic, the site delivers consistency that's an investment in user confidence. In many cases, short pages also help maintain focus, keeping to only one question or set of answers per page. This approach relies on new thinking around content design, which Sarah Richards pioneered and tested through a variety of content types.

"Good content design allows people to do or find out what they need to from government simply and quickly using the most appropriate content format available," the GDS Content Principles begin.[11] Those formats, or content types, include press releases, series of steps across pages, manuals, tables, and calculators. What became of the half-dozen articles that previously described how to calculate maternity pay? Gone! Today, GOV.UK offers a calculator in the context of a few questions, one per page. It begins with a short list of the information you'll need to have on hand, such as your salary, hiring date, and due date. When you reach the end of the questions, you have a complete, objective answer.

"People were surprised that's all they had to do," Sarah shares. User testing revealed the initial impact of that surprise: skepticism. Simplification can sometimes undermine authority, especially when people are more familiar with long-winded and circuitous government bureaucracy, medical information couched in passive voice, or academic research that leans on technical jargon to formalize shared, accepted, or intuitive practices.

To reassure users that the information they find is complete and authoritative—worthy of their confidence and trust—GDS tested new design elements, the general content design, and editorial style and tone with users.

"In the first testing we did of the new style guide, one woman looked at a [rewritten] page, squinted, and sat back," Sarah recalls. "'Is that from government?' We said yes. 'Well I don't trust it!' She Googled for another page, despite the fact that we'd started her on this page. I thought, 'No, I have to go back to the turgid language!'" Though that user was only one person, says Sarah, many others had a similar response when they viewed the shorter, more direct copy without supporting design elements. "We heard a lot of people say we were dumbing it down, it's too easy to read. But no one could act on information in the old version anyhow."

The team regrouped to test the content and editorial voice in a more real-world situation: in the context of the page design. Ben Terrett, head of design for GDS, added a banner across the top of every page, a black band with the white crown. The black-and-white linear graphic language echoes minimalism found throughout the site, but the crown gives it the mark of being official—and made all the difference. "We went from hearing 'well, I can read that' with some skepticism to 'I can read that!' with delight," Sarah says. "Otherwise, people didn't trust the new content, particularly if it was about money or benefits. We needed the crown." The crown made the more accessible, simpler copy also feel official.

Changes in typography also provided visual cues to legitimize the information and its accuracy. The early alpha version of GOV.UK used three different typefaces at a range of sizes: Gill Sans (familiar to commuters on the London Underground, which mixes Gill and Johnston Sans), Helvetica, and Georgia. Following the needs of users, who may have dyslexia or other visual issues, the team sought a new typeface that would aid reading.

"We tried lots of different ones and the best was Transport," wrote Ben on the GDS blog.[12] It was designed by Jock Kinneir and Margaret Calvert for Britain's national motorway and road sign system, which launched in 1963. "They spent years testing for legibility in all sorts of extreme conditions; in the rain, at night, at speed," he said. Fifty years later, the GDS team worked with Margaret through rounds of iteration to create new weights suitable for online readability.

"Every time they changed it, we needed to change how we wrote," Sarah explains. "With a slightly wider, really dark version, we realized we couldn't have more than four or five sentences before a big break, or it was just an assault on your eyes." It was imposing and aggressive—not the tone GOV.UK wanted to set for content that aimed to invite engagement. "We couldn't have warning boxes; they were just too heavy. And that's not people's perception of government. It was plain English but didn't look right. We also tried a really thin version of the typeface and had to write in longer paragraphs," she continues, "but it gave you a sense that it just wasn't easy to read."

Striking the appropriate balance of "grey" in density and layout is important to any brand that seeks to be authoritative and worthy of respect, but not to appear pedantic or too caught up in the details. For GOV.UK, and for most information-based or transactional websites, the text is the interface.

That interface earns trust through clear content and an appropriate look-and-feel, both working together to create repeated opportunities for success. "Repeated opportunities for success" is another way of framing a wizard, or stepped questions that offer a psychological benefit and replace a single long page. In many transaction flows, users now answer a series of questions, each with objective, simple responses, to complete a form or to drill down to receive information that is accurate and specific to their circumstances. Each step in that flow is an opportunity to build confidence: by entering information and moving along successfully, users become more certain of themselves and their own preparation—and, more broadly, more confident in the system and the content it presents. GOV.UK regained the kind of confidence that users previously found in external resources. Governments rarely boast of that kind of achievement, but as GOV.UK demonstrates, renewed confidence is a timely and necessary goal.

So is there any real difference between America's Test Kitchen and GOV.UK? The two organizations are separated

by an ocean and a topical focus—but both traffic in trust and
need to build confidence if they want to earn eyeballs.

In user experience design, we try not to slow transactions
by putting content in the checkout process that prevents
someone from completing their purchase. But brands like
America's Test Kitchen—and, for much of its web presence,
Crutchfield—aren't selling product. They're selling confidence.
More touchpoints, pages, images, and examples add fuel to
that fire. As it funnels users toward transactions and prompts
them to complete forms, GOV.UK is selling confidence as well.
But to build self-confidence—that belief you can make good
decisions because your information is current, accurate, and
actionable—"more" isn't better. It's exhausting. To act on critical information with financial, health, and civic impact, users
need to know their knowledge is complete.

"Build digital services, not websites," recommends point
eight in GOV.UK's design principles.[13] It continues:

> A service is something that helps people to do something.
> Our job is to uncover user needs, and build the service that
> meets those needs. Of course much of that will be pages on
> the web, but we're not here to build websites. The digital
> world has to connect to the real world, so we have to think
> about all aspects of a service, and make sure they add up to
> something that meets user needs.

If you aim to build services that help people, rather than
websites that serve up content, you know that you've offered
enough detail when user research and feedback reveals that

people are acting with confidence. You offer "enough" information when the detail conveys a complete story that enables users to act and feel smart about it—when they can reach the proverbial end and feel like they've caught up fully on the day's news, gained a complete understanding of how to prepare a memorable cake, or have the knowledge they need to apply for the financial benefits to which they're entitled. Complete is more important than comprehensive. As it turns out, no one has time for that or interest in it anyway.

CHAPTER 7

Balance fidelity and abstraction to inform beyond the facts

"JUST BECAUSE you're accurate doesn't mean you're interesting," jokes comedian John Mulaney in his special *Kid Gorgeous*.[1] He's talking about the irrelevance of distracting details, but his statement is a lesson to anyone trying to motivate their audience to understand and act on information. Sometimes, you have to simplify the details so that people can get the big picture and act on it. What concepts stand out as faithful to the original? That's abstraction: the process by which you transform information to simplify and translate it between the source material and the audience while remaining true to the original concepts.

Abstraction helps organizations move beyond overwhelming details to more actionable and trustworthy information. Sometimes the information you have needs to be changed into a format or set within a context that enables your audience to act. Sometimes it's too detailed to be useful, or it focuses on the wrong details. It's accurate, but not interesting, as Mulaney says. In other cases, people can't relate to the specific case to understand how it applies to them. Good advice is buried in irrelevant details. Let's explore how abstraction helps us communicate the truth with fidelity. Fidelity is the degree to which a new version reflects reality.

Do you simplify the story and leave out some details to get to the important part and retain readers? Do you shift the context to make examples more relatable and help the audience empathize? Or do you reframe details in a more familiar format, all to control the message and ensure the audience isn't distracted by the noise? Actionable communication empowers people by filtering the real world. As a designer, writer, or marketer you can provide users with the power to act with confidence. By abstracting reality, we make the essential information more actionable, useful, and personally relevant. That kind of utility is the most basic level of information design, whether your users are navigating a disease treatment plan, a ballot, or a map. By finding a balance between telling the truth and omitting unnecessary noise, you empower your audience with information that's both more useful and usable, and worthy of their trust.

"What is believed overpowers the truth," wrote Sophocles.[2] Today, perhaps, it's more accurate to say that what is believed *is* the truth. Truth is a personal thing shaped by experience and perception, but belief and truth stand separately from reality. Design is a helpful intermediary between reality and truth.

All these things are true even if they didn't happen

Abstraction allows us to act with confidence and without overthinking the details. Sometimes, writers and designers can streamline the details or condense the nuances, all in the name of serving a greater good: actionable understanding. Think about maps. Sometimes, they gloss over reality to deliver the truth.

"All maps are useful lies," offers Stanford design instructor Christina Wodtke. "A map's job is to help someone go from one place to another place. But if your map shows each restaurant, driveway, and side road accurately, it becomes so dense that you can't navigate with it." An overly detailed map won't be useful. So, maps omit details that the artist—or user, if the map is interactive—deems irrelevant. The driveways and side roads still exist; they just aren't shown. In some cases, details are exaggerated to reflect importance. In other cases, the cartographer changes relationships to serve a greater purpose: the map doesn't just need to be useful, but it needs to be usable— memorable, even. It needs to fit the user's mental model.

Information architecture pioneer Richard Saul Wurman designed a map[3] of two major Tokyo subway lines that crisply contrasts against models that are more representative. Like in standard maps of the city's transit system, the circular Yamanote Line rings the city and the Chūō-Sōbu Line bisects the ring. There's a jog in the middle, with the lines shifting further north as they go east. But Wurman smooths the turns— committing lies of omission—and broadens the ring. His map is usable, though it's not realistic. But do these changes matter on a map? "Underground, you don't need to know every turn," comments Christina. "They don't matter. Instead, Wurman made a concept model of the subway based on a yin-yang. When people familiar with a yin-yang see his map, they update their mental model of the subway system." Wurman's choices matter because his model helps visitors remember the relationships between stations and learn approximate distances, contributing to their confidence and trust that they can get around.

But models are not without their baggage. As communication theorist Paul Watzlawick noted,[4] we cannot *not* communicate. To western tourists, the model may be helpful—but to others, the yin-yang as a graphic element, divorced of its meaning of dualism, just feels like reductive, clichéd orientalism.

"Mental models help people remember and attain new information," continues Christina. That process is vital for giving people ownership over their learning and confidence in their own ability to self-educate.

When we abstract ideas to aid attention, comprehension, and retention—the process of learning that Christina describes as her "teaching trifecta"—those ideas have more impact. We remove the friction of unnecessary details and sticking points. If TED champions "ideas worth spreading," abstraction and simplification enable that spread. "Look at info memes," says Christina. "They're models so small and easy to draw that they can travel. They're simple enough that when you're talking to your boss, you can grab a whiteboard marker and throw it up there." These concepts are so simple that they can be sketched and passed on without losing information.

Map design offers a compelling example of the ethics of abstraction that span the distance between a daunting, overly

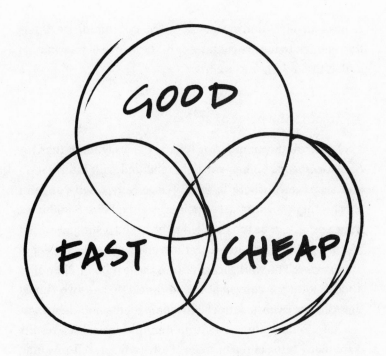

FIGURE 7.1 Whether you're citing the account manager's triad of "good, fast, or cheap—you can pick two!" to a client or evaluating maturity against Maslow's hierarchy, some concepts are simple enough to sketch that they don't lose information through retelling.

detailed reality and an actionable truth. Sometimes information is too detailed to be actionable.

"Information anxiety is the black hole between data and knowledge, and it happens when information doesn't tell us what we want or need to know," wrote Wurman.[5] Maps help reduce that anxiety for some people. They tell us where we are, where we can go, and how to get there. Maps abstract reality by sacrificing some detail to be more useful. That tradeoff reduces anxiety—and anxiety is the killer of confidence. But is that enough to inspire confidence in the source of information and, ultimately, to inspire trust?

Abstract to the point of action

In chapter four, you met April Starr, the designer of the Cancer Worksheets. "When you're bombarded with information and aren't sure where to focus—especially when you're in shock—they pull out the key points," she explains. Sometimes, information can be too detailed to be useful, especially when it's coming from multiple directions and lacks a clear order of importance. The worksheets resolve that problem: they offer a focal point for conversations and next steps—two things that can get easily sidetracked when patients and their families have to navigate orders from multiple specialists, results from many tests, and a barrage of advice from well-meaning friends and support organizations.

"People send a million links to check out *this* resource and *that* resource—and that's not good," April says. "It's overwhelming! We know, when you're in shock, you'll make more mistakes. It's tough to listen. The worksheet gives you something to focus on. When you're in shock, you get tunnel vision. So where do you focus? Here. The worksheets give you the basics." With the essential information about the diagnosis, tests, and game plan, patients and their families can become more active participants in treatment. While initial diagnosis can rob someone of their sense of control, this tool meets them where they are to renew a sense of confidence and empower them again, with everything they need on a single sheet of paper.

Participation in decision making is some of the most vital and affirming action for people with acute and serious illness. The Cancer Worksheets omit some details and condense others in the interest of empowering patients and their families to be more active participants in the short term—and gain a more comprehensive and educated understanding of treatment and prognosis in the long term. Like a good map, the Cancer Worksheets tell people where they are, where they can go, and how to get there.

Abstraction can help us understand the big picture more quickly, which can often jumpstart more confident action. For decades, students across the US and Canada have put their faith in CliffsNotes, the summaries of hundreds of books by authors from Chinua Achebe to Émile Zola. Though they purport to complement the source material, CliffsNotes often act as a streamlined replacement when it's crunch time and an essay is due. That's when summarized information can help. Readers put faith in the analysis of others to develop their own perspective with confidence.

When you offer people the agency to self-educate and learn, they gain two things: knowledge and self-confidence. Abstraction can help elevate concepts so people can act on information without getting bogged down by the details. By abstracting knowledge to the right degree—neither glossing over it in a superficial way nor miring readers in minutiae— they can build on success to gain confidence in a process, service, or organization. People don't need details if they understand the lesson, and the lesson they internalize is formative: success drives trust.

Offer enough detail to be plausible but leave space to be relatable

Abstraction offers another benefit: by sacrificing detail, the essence of your message becomes plausible. Good storytellers give us enough detail to see what they mean, but ensure that those details are relatable enough to be relevant to the audience. The empathy of shared experience orients us and fills the space between the storyteller's narrative and how we relate it to our own adventures in the world. "Stories are good audio maps," says Christina Wodtke. They focus your attention, facilitate comprehension, and aid retention—or our ability to organize new information into the concepts we already grasp. At the most basic level, metaphors work in the same way: they offer a shorthand mental model that anyone can relate to their own experiences and things they already know. "The project was a rollercoaster" conveys the abrupt highs and lows of an assignment, even though the team never set foot in an amusement park. "That presentation was a slog" calls to mind trudging through a muddy hike or slushy winter sidewalk, even though everyone sat through it without getting out of their seats. Fidelity to the details matters far less than the point: that presentation was tiring, arduous, and took forever! You're lucky you didn't have to sit through it.

When you cut distracting details, empathy fills that gap—but empathy is more than a byproduct of minimalist design or concise writing. It's a core product—and a Trojan horse for trust. By allowing space for the audience to overlay their own memories on a story or image, you make the information more valuable to them, because now it's more relevant. Realtors apply this method when they stage a home, leaving a few inviting landscape paintings but hiding the personal vacation photos. They keep the details that illustrate specific common experiences, but cut the bits that prevent prospective buyers from seeing themselves in the space. Moreover, they retain the décor and furniture that hints at relatable lifestyle aspirations and adequate storage.

Abstraction is different from generalizing. Don't cut the details that convey central concepts and core truths, or there won't be anything that the audience can relate to their own lives. While illustrations and stories are no substitute for data, they help us connect with bigger concepts. Those concepts can feel familiar if they relate to our own experiences, and it feels safe to build new knowledge on familiar concepts. We use data, but we *trust* humans. By sharing enough specific detail, you can ground the truth and key takeaways in concepts familiar enough to encourage your audience's trust and interest.

When imagery or content focuses too much on the wrong details, viewers lose the bigger concepts. Airbnb's early work with video tours offered too much detail. They painstakingly gathered all the features visitors look for in search queries— hairdryer! laundry on site!—and went overboard showing each of these details, which could have come through just as well in bulleted lists. Video tours were well produced, but it was too much. Their professional polish and scripted content made them informative—but they didn't feel authentic.

"Our early videos were minute-long stories that reflected common search queries," explains Shawn Sprockett, a former design lead at Airbnb. "They were beautifully shot and well produced—but the way they answered questions looked like marketing." The scripted, anticipatory manner of fully explaining house listings proactively answered questions for prospective guests, but the videos came on too hard. "They made the listings look less authentic," he adds. Rather than looking like the work of real people showing off their apartments or vacation rentals, the videos looked and sounded slick. They were driven by search engine terms, not property owners' passion for their town or pride in a newly remodeled kitchen. All that polished content overwhelmed potential guests and property owners and put them in a defensive mindset, pushing them to move on to other listings and other rental sites.

"The next version of those videos looked more real," he continues. The hosts focused on the details they thought were important and filmed without format guidelines or keyword lists from Airbnb. "No more scripting—we had people just answer questions in their own words." Gone was the professional camerawork, or at least the qualities that hinted at it. Instead of reminding hosts to film with the camera in a horizontal orientation, they let them hold the camera or phone vertically, the default for most people who don't have a background in photography. "We rotated from horizontal cinematic filming to vertical, like Snapchat," he says. That change might make some photographers cringe, but it speaks the language of people who aren't professionals and just want to grab a snapshot or shoot a quick video. It's more relatable and authentic. "Authenticity builds trust, and we don't want to undercut our own goals," Shawn notes. The details that came through revealed more of the hosts' passion and less of user search queries.

The simple change of switching from horizontal to vertical in the videos signaled that the values of the person (or brand) making the video may be more aligned with the values of visitors who don't care about such details, or are more attuned to Snapchat than to professional videography. By focusing attention elsewhere and seemingly letting those details slip through the cracks, Airbnb affects a younger, more digital-native-friendly posture. Here, authenticity builds on a carefully studied apathy.

"We never intentionally made anything look bad," cautions Shawn. "But we realized that something that looks great to a designer could just get in the way." By considering the finer points in camerawork and content creation, Airbnb created something more accessible and useful to a potential guest.

One of Airbnb's central motivations is to help travelers connect more meaningfully with their destinations. If you're looking outside of standard, generic hotel chains for something more authentic, a homestay through Airbnb offers interaction with local hosts and the comfort of a home. By focusing on details like video that maintains the voice and style of hosts, Airbnb ensures that their production style doesn't distract from the main points of their value proposition to visitors.

Consider which details are necessary to drive action

"Democracy is a design problem. The centerpiece of solving that problem is ensuring voter intent through design," explains the Center for Civic Design.[6] Voter intent—the process of ensuring a ballot is marked and counted as the voter intended—is confounded by logistics, disenfranchisement, and confusing and inconsistent communication. These issues compound the challenges of maintaining and communicating election security, something that is key to maintaining voters' trust in the process. More detailed information and precise communication doesn't always fuel greater understanding, trust, or participation.

"We don't need government brutalism!" explains Whitney Quesenbery, director of the Center for Civic Design. Instead of copy that reads YOUR BALLOT MUST BE RETURNED BY 8 PM ON ELECTION DAY, the text should read *Please return your ballot by 8 PM on election day.* "It's still an official tone, but it's friendly, not aggressive," she says. Whitney has overseen the Center's projects to research and design best practices for election design across the country, including California's Voter Bill of Rights, vote-by-mail forms, and voting systems. The "official tone" she describes omits some of the precise technical language of government in exchange for more conversational engagement that buries some details and contextualizes others.

"We can't avoid using terminology like 'residence' on forms," she explains. But it can be put into a more familiar context. "We can ask 'where do you live (residence address)?' or 'where do you live as your official residence?'" Much like the plain language work of the NHS, the process of unpacking jargon on voter registration forms helps to meet people where they are while couching official terminology in an accessible context.

Same-day voter registration presented challenges of both jargon and complexity. For citizens who miss the deadline to register or need to update their voter registration information, it allows them to still cast a vote in an election—their ballot is processed and counted after the county elections office completes the voter registration verification process. In California, it's officially known as "conditional voter registration," and while the process is simple, it can be complex to articulate in full detail. Those details might dissuade a voter or make them ask if the effort is really worth it. But the internal process doesn't affect them, so the details don't need to either.

Following guidance from the Center for Civic Design, messaging about same-day voter registration in California no longer leads with the label and explanation of "conditional voter registration." Instead the details are explained in an FAQ. "The point isn't what it's called, but that California offers it and how to use it," says Whitney.

Details can sometimes introduce suspicion into a process that's already fraught with questions, but minimal phrasing that glosses over procedure can undermine confidence too. In Colorado, the Arapahoe County Clerk's Office ran into that issue with the 2015 election, a vote-at-home system. The paper ballots featured stubs containing information in a 2D QR code that helped ensure each voter got the right packet, depending on if they were overseas, needed to provide ID, or had other requirements. When voters returned their ballots, they needed to remove the stub to ensure secrecy—but few did. "'Tear off stub' made people think they were being encouraged to invalidate the ballot," Whitney says. Voters called the Clerk's Office with concerns that their ballot would be flagged or identified, or disqualified entirely. Simple language left them in the dark.

"We were trying to use plain language—and it backfired on us!" says Jennifer Morrell, deputy of elections and recording for Arapahoe County. "We're an all-mail ballot state. Depending on the election, more than 90% of registered voters will mail in a ballot, with the remaining voters coming in to same-day register or vote. One of the bottlenecks for us is opening ballots; it's a human process. Folks get trays of 100 envelopes and have to pull a secrecy sleeve out of the envelope, then the ballot out of the secrecy sleeve, and make sure there aren't any marks like coffee stains that would prevent scanning. Then they have to tear the ballot stub." The county had wanted to streamline that process by asking voters to remove the stubs, which not only slowed down the process but also heaped up in giant bins and caused paper dust to choke the offices. "We have to stop, backfold the perforation a few times, then carefully tear it off. If we could shave time off each ballot that we open, across 400,000 ballots... that's a lot!" she notes.

For the primary in June 2016, the county added the all-caps text "VOTER: PLEASE REMOVE THIS BALLOT STUB," only to see even more ballots come back with the stub still attached. "People were calling our hotline asking if there was some sort of conspiracy," Jennifer says. They wondered if someone was trying to violate the secrecy of the ballots. Though the effort streamlined an administrative process, to many voters it seemed suspicious.

"After talking with Whitney, we decided to include instructions and reasons. Just for fun, we also decided to print the image of our 'I voted' sticker on the stub too, since people don't get a sticker when they vote by mail," she continues. By the general election in November 2016, the ballots included more detailed content. That copy abstracts the process of how QR codes correlate voting materials with specific voters and allow for a faster mailing process, but it hits the important details of what it is and why it matters.

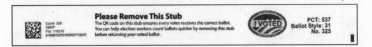

FIGURE 7.2 The final November 2016 version of the Arapahoe County ballot package instruction slip explains the QR code and why voters need to remove the stub before casting a vote.

"The QR code on this stub ensures every voter receives the correct ballot. You can help election workers count ballots quicker by removing this stub before returning your voted ballot," it reads. When ballots started coming in, nearly all the stubs had been removed.

"You need to learn what voters need to know to trust the information," Jennifer told her team with the Center for Civic Design. What voters needed to know was why, not how—and that was enough to help them build a clearer mental model and understand the process. That understanding let them feel more confident about the system, so they could invest their trust and act on the information.

Build on the familiar to maintain confidence

Much like how Wurman used a familiar icon to reference Tokyo on a map, we can abstract information and make it more accessible. Translating information into a more familiar context or format can help rein in the audience's attention. When formats are familiar they become invisible, one less thing vying for attention. Moreover, when the audience already trusts the construct, the new information it presents can inherit some of that trust by association.

Alexandra Chandler used a familiar construct to make the complex simple to deliver emotionally charged and politically contentious information in the workplace.[7] In 2006, she transitioned and became the first transgender person to serve in the Office of Naval Intelligence. She had served two years as a civilian intelligence analyst, where she focused on weapons of mass destruction, then moved up through division chief of maritime counterproliferation, serving more than a decade in the US Department of Defense. Her career in the intelligence community was marked by citations for meritorious service, commendations for leadership, and high team morale—but it was abstracted communication in familiar contexts that made all of that possible.

Shortly after Alexandra came out and announced her plan to start presenting at work as a woman, rumors started to swirl in her department. "At a town hall about the Navy's pay-for-performance system, there was an open period for questions," she remembers. "Suddenly, someone asked if a 'drag queen' would be allowed to use the bathroom." The moment was arresting for Alexandra, who had stayed behind at her desk to keep working but was listening in remotely. "I felt friends silently come up behind me to put their hands on my shoulder to support me," she recalls. "I heard the CO take the question and respond. He explained that I was an exemplary employee, who he knew and respected, and who was going through a medical procedure. 'And yes, she will use the bathroom,' he stated firmly. 'This is about taking care of our people, and Navy values of courage, commitment, and mission. I've given an order and it is final.'" His message was simple, clear, and grounded in the consistency of shared values—and it reflected the communication plan Alexandra had put in place.

"When I transitioned, I was uniform in how I approached my explanation. Whether people were more senior or junior, I was concerned with the consistency of the narrative they heard," she explains. "Everyone got the same details: 'this is a medical process and I have been taking hormones,' and I wanted to keep to that line lest there be any confusion." Alexandra worried that even supportive colleagues might grow concerned about the impact of her transition on them. "If people were afraid that this process would put demands on them, like to learn one name one day, another the next, or that it would cause confusion in our workplace, I wanted to make sure everyone was operating off the same script. So when questions would come, I would always answer in the same level of detail. I'd set the bar on the kind of language I'd use from the start."

The language she used in oral and written communication to brief her team echoed the style and level of detail of intelligence briefings and information memos. That structure was something familiar and trustworthy to her audience. They knew to expect concrete details about what would come next, when events would take place, who to look to for further information, and the process for reporting. Alexandra introduced the information about her transition the same way, in a briefing she called Compartment T.

"I didn't go so far in making the plan feel like an intelligence product as to use classification markings, but I provided a clear risk assessment," she describes. "I told the management chain the story of how my transition would play out: on this day, this happens. The structure was an executive summary, the facts we know, what we're going to have to assess, what are our needs." In that familiar format, she detailed communications support she might require and possible threats to existing relationships with more conservative policy makers.

"When we think about gender, it bundles up so many assumptions about the experiences of a lifetime. So when you come out, you're not only introducing new data. This person you had in one box is no longer in that box, and in fact is moving from one box to another!" She explained the challenge of conveying new information and asking people to rethink their organization of that information on a cold February day to a crowd gathered in Boston for World Information Architecture Day 2018. Her audience was already attuned to the challenges of making complex data useful and accessible, though few were familiar with the layered complexities of military culture, gender transition, and information security. "When one comes out in a personal life context, it's often done with storytelling and appeals to emotion and shared connection. 'Have you always just felt like a woman? Well, I have too, and now I'm making myself congruent with that!' And you talk about what's going to come next, when you'll start using those pronouns—and that's how it's done in our personal lives," Alexandra told the audience.

But coming out in a professional setting is different. Coming out in the intelligence community—and a military organization in the intelligence community—presented the common challenges shared by any organization trying to engage stakeholders in sensitive information that demands consistency, clarity, and multiple people managing its rollout.

"I tried to model my storytelling after the environment we were in," Alexandra explains. "In the intelligence community, we talk about compartments: sensitive, compartmentalized information. I came to call this 'Compartment T'—T for transgender. That way, I could have a little shorthand even for talking with people in the office. When it came time to talk to the leadership about it, I didn't want to just talk about how I felt. I came up with an 'information memo' with a P, O, A, and M—Plan of Action and Milestones. We invited coworkers to a special 'read-in,' which is what you do to get access to new, sensitive compartmentalized information." A numbered copy of the letter greeted each person attending, and the group treated the information in the same manner they would speak about intelligence information: *Here's the information—now how are we going to protect it?* "It was 2006, and the only way I could make the transition work was with an understanding that I didn't want it to be public— and the chain of command wouldn't want that either. I just wanted to keep doing my job. So we protected it in a structure that people were familiar with. We talk about releasability a lot in the intelligence community. How much is releasable to which partners? What do we do with our foreign partners? What do we do with political appointees we're briefing in the Pentagon? Who tells them, when, and how, and who prepares the brief for that? And standard operating procedures: when does my email get changed? When does my nameplate change? That was Compartment T."

Any message can benefit from using familiar constructs that control the audience's expectations. A familiar format means there's one less thing to distract attention or raise concerns. While we abstract information to translate it for better use by the audience, the process of fitting it to familiar structures, styles, and formats walks a fine line. Alexandra didn't dress up the information memo with the seals and graphics that might normally accompany a briefing; she didn't want to pander to colleagues or undermine the gravity of the message. But by reducing the details to the facts and familiar structure of the context, she made her story actionable. Her team maintained confidence in her communication and that they wouldn't be hit with surprises about the impact of her transition. They knew when to expect answers to specific questions and gained confidence in their ability to self-educate at a time when the topic of gender transition was often guarded and off the table. She presented the big picture and key concepts while abstracting the extraneous or irrelevant personal details, maintaining high fidelity to the main message as she delivered it to different audiences.

Whether you're designing a map, confronting sensitive communication, or planning a trip, the devil is in the details— and the truth is in our ability to distill those details. The right amount of detail ensures your audience believes your story and can relate it to their own needs. Thoughtful omissions, by mapmakers, form designers, and other storytellers, allow the audience to focus on what's most important. And familiar constructs reduce the cognitive load surrounding new or sensitive topics. By understanding these principles of abstraction, you can filter, prioritize, and simplify information so the audience can act on it and trust that it's true to the original intent.

Relevance and fidelity are empowering; these qualities drive our trust in content, tools, experts, and organizations. Whether it's a preferred news network, product review website, or a friend who always has the best restaurant recommendations, we trust sources that give us information that's useful and accurate. If information is power, it's because confidence in our own knowledge fuels trust.

(III)

Vulnerability

VULNERABILITY REFERS to the uncertainty that comes with exposing yourself to risk in the hope of finding a greater reward. Your brand is vulnerable when you seek out community and risk attracting criticism in the hopes of improving, finding their support, or connecting with people who share your values. Your brand is even more vulnerable in the aftermath of missteps, scandal, or other screwups, and you seek to recover with transparency, accountability, and grace. You risk public scorn and further criticism, but with humility, you can gain renewed loyalty and trust.

Smart organizations embrace the opportunity in humility, opening themselves to the insight and criticism of others. They don't just listen but also incorporate feedback. Design your business and communication to welcome and apply input. Does that exposure feel uncomfortable, even vulnerable? In asking for audience input, startups share questions they can't yet answer, and reveal gaps in their vision. By exposing research in progress, scientists acknowledge what they don't yet know. But that show of vulnerability isn't weakness. Grounded in humility and framed as an opportunity for greater good, evolution, and growth, vulnerability is a strength. Vulnerability trades the safety of sure bets and certainty for choices that open us and our organizations to risk—and greater rewards. So what if everyone's a critic, or if feedback slows progress? Together with their critics and customers, brands that embrace vulnerability go far—and with humility, they grow stronger, forgoing the speed of launch for the support of an informed, invested community.

CHAPTER 8

Convene community for collaborative creation

To go fast, go alone.
To go far, go together.

SMART BUSINESS owners and marketers go far because they go together. They gather wisdom from the community by engaging with vulnerability and openness. Value isn't only the product of independent genius design. If you believe that form follows function, first deliver on function: meet the needs of your users. To make things that serve your community, involve your community. It takes vulnerability to step down off a pedestal or out from behind the curtain and engage your users by eliciting input, not merely encouraging comments or sharing. It takes an unwavering sense of purpose to declare the polarizing perspectives that are core to your organization—but a more loyal and engaged community is the reward for that risk. Your organization will need to be vulnerable enough to show itself: what it knows, what it needs, and what it believes. Your audience will get to know your brand, faults and all. Don't worry about losing their respect; if you do it right, your brand will *demonstrate* respect and earn it in return. People will see themselves better reflected in what you create—together.

> *To go fast, go alone.*
> *To go far, go together.*

Communities teach us that it's time to tack on an addendum to that aphorism: *To go well, go humbly.* To go in the right direction, to go with clear vision and purpose, humble yourself to the wisdom and input of others. Humility strengthens us—and it can strengthen our organizations, brands, and governmental institutions as well.

Break the fourth wall to meet your audience where they are

An invested community is what *The New York Times* seeks to build around its hallmark human interest stories. As a national newspaper of record and home to more Pulitzer Prizes than any other newspaper, the *Times* strives to inform readers and cultivate an empathetic understanding of the world. To tell an accurate story, the *Times* needs readers to inform the reporting.

For many marketers, the relationship between producers and consumers is set in stone: organizations produce content and their audiences consume it. Social media offers the opportunity to cultivate more interaction around content, but like the comments section in a newspaper, it often creates more work for brands to both create content and engage with comments, even while working in the constraints of limited character counts and other platform restrictions. What could it look like for organizations to really break the fourth wall? Rather than limit audience engagement to commentary on content, what would it look like for you to engage customers in content creation itself?

Collaborative creation shapes coverage of racism and race-related issues in Chicago in *The New York Times*. *Race/Related* is the *Times'* special newsletter about race, comprising reporting, commentary, polling, and art. When *Race/Related* turned its focus to Chicago, the resulting content was a product shaped both by and for its subject.

"With *Race/Related*, we created a feedback loop," explains Antonio de Luca, *The New York Times'* visual editor on the project. "We asked the public a series of questions and then served the answers back to them so they could see the reflection of their input. Then we based our stories on those questions." The newsletter incorporated further feedback as featured comments and continued to survey readers to orient its focus—and to ensure that the reporting built rapport with the audience.

"The process helped the public understand that we're in a discourse together," he says. "Discourse" implies a conversation, talking through the situation not to report on what is, but to dig deeper and come to a greater understanding. It's also the meaningful, informative conversation so many brands crave and seek out through the formal mediation of focus groups. *The New York Times* demonstrated that collaborative creation can both attract and foster a sense of community around the product: more comprehensive reporting.

Antonio describes how the conversation that grew helped people understand that the *Times* wasn't talking at them, but instead wanted to reflect a bigger picture by cultivating their input and talking *with* them. "Perhaps from this work, people saw they can talk to each other, too," he notes. For a product designed to further understanding of race in America, that's a noble goal.

Create a safe space for input and a brave space to build together

The "Hyphen-Nation" project allowed the *Times* to adopt an even more open stance: rather than listening and reporting through co-creation with the community, the newspaper

FIGURE 8.1 With "Hyphen-Nation," *The New York Times* offers a platform for community and a conduit for their content.

functioned more as a conduit for the voices of their audience and subjects.

"'Hyphen-Nation' speaks to how this country comprises immigrants who come here and become more 'hybrid' individuals," explains Antonio. The project spotlights the stories of American citizens who struggle to relate to a country that alternates between celebrating and demonizing the immigrant experience. A series of videos featuring an array of first-person anecdotes about identity in the American experience came to life with the scrawling, relatable illustration style of Josh Cochran. "We used illustration to give the sense that it's these people illustrating their memories, and transcend time periods and how people view things," Antonio says. *"The New York Times* is a great reflection of New York City: some things are quite liberal and always changing. Compare it to a German paper that reflects the national sensibility—it's more perfect but cold. Here, the kind of artwork we commission reflects New York." Rougher lines, collage-like compositions, and less precision create a more approachable and familiar feel.

A hand-wrought visual style that demonstrates human creativity helps encourage more people to get involved: the bulk of content in "Hyphen-Nation" actually comes from reader testimonials. "People sent us video selfies about what it means to be Japanese-American, Afghan-American, et cetera," Antonio says. "And we embraced the errors." They didn't fix typos in user-submitted content. The vulnerability of including original user content, warts and all, helps invite greater participation and understanding. "The reader remembers the human being on the other side of the device when we strip away the perfection. Empathy and participation: that's community."

FIGURE 8.2 Illustrations from the website of the German news-paper *Frankfurter Allgemeine Zeitung*, by Andre Piron, and in "Hyphen-Nation," by Josh Cochran.

The New York Times trades vulnerability for community by exposing its gaps in knowledge, inviting collaboration, and creating a non-intimidating forum for participation. Drawing on the catchphrase of disability activism, the *Times* embraced the cause of "nothing about us without us." First, they recognized gaps in the staff's cultural awareness. Then they sought to create a more meaningful dialogue and richer product by centering the readers their coverage addressed. They structured content creation to avoid doing anything that affected readers without involving the readers they would affect. To meet that goal, the team embraced a humble, vulnerable perspective that drives the work of journalism, as well as any kind of user experience design: they had to acknowledge that their personal experience was no substitute for understanding their subjects' experience. But editorial arrogance can mask a bigger issue. Their knowledge and personal experience may prevent a team from understanding what topics are of importance to their audience. By realizing these two challenges, the *Times* opened themselves up to be swayed by voices beyond their assignment editors. They humbly acknowledged the limits of their worldview to create a broader understanding of our world.

Humble yourself and move beyond design thinking and empathy to respect

For Silicon Valley startups that address only the wealthy male problems of Silicon Valley, humility and the input of community can be a differentiating strength. That differentiation is part of the allure of "design thinking," the philosophy and methodology evangelized most prominently by design consultancy IDEO. Corporations often chase design thinking as a plug-and-play differentiator: adopt a mindset that prizes creative confidence, user needs, and boldly divergent thinking over the handcuffs of process, budget, and history, and you can be confident your team will solve problems more effectively. Go forth and disrupt, young man.

Design thinking done well demands time and deep attention. "It requires systems thinking: realizing that any problem is part of a larger whole, and that the solution is likely to require understanding the entire system," wrote design researcher Don Norman in a 2010 article called "Design Thinking: A Useful Myth."[1] But in application, framed by agile methodology and a rush to market, design thinking often doesn't look like that.

In companies that pursue a superficial implementation of design thinking, the process lacks rigor, depth of experience, and the investment of time to first set the right foundation: teams may solve problems creatively and effectively, but they may not be the *right* problems. Only by forging respectful relationships with our audiences can we properly understand the problems we need to solve. Relationships and community take time to build—the thing often in shortest supply at even the most well-funded startups. They also demand something else: vulnerability. When brands go out on a limb to speak in a natural voice, reveal political passions, and spend time letting their customers get to know corporate vision and product roadmaps, they risk alienating portions of the audience. They risk scorn from the media, and they risk angry boycotts. But the reward for trading generic and cool detachment for

a more human and passionate perspective is deeper relationships with the core audience. Brands also build empathy, not
through user research or dilettante engagement of consulting, but through deep and direct experience as part of that
community.

Empathy is a casual and common catchphrase of user-
centered design. Among designers and researchers, it's code
for differentiating from a more traditional approach of brand-
driven design. But just because we focus equally on the needs
of users and the companies working to sell to them, it doesn't
mean we necessarily empathize with them—indeed, it might
be a new kind of arrogance to think so.

"I can't stand the word 'empathy,'" says April Starr, designer
of the Cancer Worksheets. As a student, she focused on
design thinking and user-centered design at Carnegie Mellon's School of Design, one of the best undergraduate design
programs in the world. She cut her teeth conducting user
research at E-Lab, guided experience research for projects at
Motorola, led projects and shaped the human factors community at IDEO, and taught service design and user research
on the faculty at Illinois Institute of Technology's Institute
of Design. All of her professional and academic experience is
framed by a belief in empathy as the bedrock of user research.
And then, she suffered profound loss not by designing for it,
but through personal experience.

"No one can empathize with me, and even when I hear what
others have gone through, it's not empathy because their loss
is personal," she says. Illness, death, and grief are common
and unifying, but entirely specific and unique to each individual and their survivors. "So when designers say empathy,

we're being flip. We can't know everything. But there are other things we can do to help," April explains.

Compassion calls us to help, not because we can truly know and understand another's experience, but because we respect and appreciate them just the same. Empathy requires that we try to understand how an experience is for someone else, instead of assuming that their experience is identical to our own. For marketers to empathize with a broad audience with diverse experiences is impossible; beyond that, it's presumptuous. But we can always approach our audiences with respect, interest, and the humility to better understand their needs. In *Race/Related* and "Hyphen-Nation," *The New York Times* team humbled itself to create a community for other voices, designing the tools and visual language that felt familiar and safe for sharing. With the Cancer Worksheets, April created a similar space to invite sharing, encourage conversation between patients and healthcare providers, and foster more patient involvement.

"It's arrogant of the design field to claim you can achieve empathy by spending an hour in an observation. Instead, involve those people in the process," April says. Her call to design practitioners applies to physicians as well as they attempt to solve problems by treating the whole patient—a sort of systems thinking at the human scale. Patients can find a more caring and supportive experience when they're involved in their own healthcare, rather than just being recipients of a service that may not fully acknowledge their specific needs and deeper goals.

By putting in the time to nurture community and bring your readers, consumers, users, or clients close—by breaking that old boundary between producer and consumer—you run the risk of exposing your inexperience and lack of knowledge. But the cost of going to market with an inapplicable or tone-deaf solution is far greater than the ego and control you give up.

Show yourself and risk everything, with immeasurable rewards

Brands also build community by exposing their activism and putting a stake in the ground for social causes. Of course, in choosing to do so they risk politicizing a previously milquetoast brand—but by defining who they are, what they support, and what they stand for, they can draw an even broader and more loyal community, attracted not just by their products but by their politics.

In 2016, Penzeys Spices chose to leave the innocuous middle ground of selling pepper blends and other kitchen mainstays to make clear their corporate politics on racism, marriage equality, gun safety, and immigration policy. Penzeys celebrates cooking as an expression of love, community, and culture. Cooking makes meals from vegetables, meat, and various carbohydrates—and from human migration, spices sourced from regions at war, and other not-so-apolitical topics. In that context, Bill Penzey, owner of the largest independent spice retailer in the US, uses the company's platform to advocate for many issues, including immigration-friendly policies—and a White House populated by a more immigration-friendly president.

Bill Penzey has long used his company's spice catalogue to weave in personal opinions in support of teachers and in opposition to racism in sports and media. Shortly after the 2016 presidential election, he embraced a bigger platform for bigger topics. He emailed customers and posted to the company's Facebook page about "the open embrace of racism by the Republican Party."[2] The post was shared more than 4,000 times in the first week. More posts and emails followed, going viral as Bill's community of fans expanded beyond home cooks to others who shared his frustration and politics.

At the same time, Penzeys' closest competitor in their home state of Wisconsin took a different stance. Patty and Tom Erd, owners of The Spice House and Bill Penzey's sister and brother-in-law, offered a discount code of NOPOLITICS. "My husband and I are very careful to never bring politics or personal opinions into our spice company, they have no business there," Patty Erd posted. That stance reflects a distance and privilege not shared by people affected by discriminatory policy, so a gambit to stay out of politics is a political statement in itself. Now home cooks have a clearer choice about the community they choose to support.

Penzeys' activism has had an impact on its community, and it's not without risk. Following Bill Penzey's post-election email, the company saw a 3% drop in customers—but more than a 50% increase in online sales.[3] As more people shared his posts, they saw themselves as part of the movement and supported the company with orders as gifts, even if they themselves didn't cook.

Penzeys' activism risks losing market share but fosters a loyal community, as demonstrated in record sales.

By going out on a limb, they make it safe for their community of supporters to talk about their politics too. And the

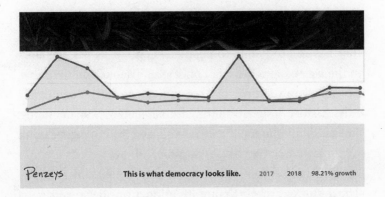

Penzeys   **This is what democracy looks like.**   2017   2018   98.21% growth

FIGURE 8.3 Sales in 2017, represented by the lower line, were relatively flat. Sales in 2018, represented by the mountainous upper line, were more dramatic, driving 98% growth at Penzeys. The spikes occur in the wake of the brand's most popular political posts.

spice merchant isn't alone. Over the past five years, support for brand activism has remained high and steady. Global Strategy Group's annual business and politics study consistently reports that roughly 80% of survey respondents voice agreement that brands should participate in social activism.[4] "There is a reward for companies that take action on political and social issues, and a penalty for inaction," reports the 2019 study, in which more neutral brands are described as "untrustworthy." More than 60% of survey respondents voiced support for companies taking a position on immigration reform in particular.

Community is a powerful tool for brands to share their inner workings or deepest beliefs. This type of engagement takes time and the willingness to be vulnerable, but demonstrates respect for the audience of engaged consumers and brand fans. Organizations like *The New York Times* build community to create a richer, more representative product that has clearer value to people. Their works fits elegantly in the user experience triad of "useful, usable, and desirable," developed 30 years ago by Liz Sanders,[5] an early champion of participatory design. By letting the subjects of human interest stories shape the focus of those stories, and bringing more voices into the reporting, *The New York Times* tells a better story—but also uses its imprimatur to expand the canon of whose stories are worth our attention. Consider the value of vulnerability in your organization: by acknowledging gaps in knowledge and expanding your research to bring prospective users into the process of creation, not only can you create a product more suited to their needs, you can also help those needs become more valid in the broader industry.

Validating perspectives is a core part of community build-ing. For brands like Penzeys, Patagonia, Qantas, Danone, The Body Shop, and countless others, activism in support of LGBTQ rights, environmental action, immigration, and racial justice doesn't drive away community, but instead helps attract it. In 2018, the Edelman Earned Brand study reported that 64% of consumers worldwide indicated that they will avoid or buy a brand based on its position on a social or political issue.[6]

This activity goes beyond once-a-year donations. For many customers, it's not enough to see the brands they buy engage in anodyne pinkwashing in the name of breast cancer aware-ness every October; in fact, that kind of brief and superficial support attracts ire and may turn away more customers than it attracts. Consumer response reveals their keen interest in learning about the deeper passions that drive organizations and their leaders. Indeed, in the face of organizations like Qantas, ANZ Bank, and the Australian Football League leading a vocal charge for marriage equality in Australia, brands that step back from the community in the name of neutrality risk even greater backlash. Coopers Brewery tested that approach, releasing ads that showed a lighter, "above the fray" perspective on staying out of politics. Their neutral stance was met by pub boycotts until they finally reversed position and affirmed support for Australian marriage equality.[7] In hiding politics and the human perspectives that our organizations comprise, we can still fire up a community, but it may not be one that supports the goals and growth we have in mind.

Closed organizations, with secretive processes and silence in the face of social issues, may face a risk far greater than they understand. By hiding away, they shield themselves from criticism—but they also don't open themselves to the benefits of community. Denying your weaknesses surfaces a different kind of vulnerability: you risk being ignored and abandoned by audiences who have more pressing concerns. Instead, humble yourself, engage your audience, and show them who you are—so you can move forward together.

CHAPTER 9

Lean into the lessons of what went wrong

IT'S RISKY for a brand to put a stake in the ground, but it takes even more vulnerability to acknowledge deficiencies and ask for help. Perhaps your company screwed up and employees, critics, and customers are demanding an explanation and accountability. Is that portrait of vulnerability painfully familiar? Your organization is at its most vulnerable when you're staggering away from mistakes, wounded by errors of judgment, and reeling from jaw-dropping calamities. Whether blame is broad or focused like a spear, what comes next matters most. Do you double down on defeat, or do you embrace opportunity?

Many companies double down on bad behavior. Perhaps the CEO speaks without thinking, the company is caught supporting discriminatory legislation, or they flout safety regulations. If they just choose to ignore the situation and hope bad press blows over, they're in for a surprise. The problems continue when they fail to acknowledge, apologize, and change their behavior. They lose customers and market share, and rightfully earn our disdain. But disdain is not a good teacher; we learn more from admirable lessons of organizations who grow stronger by openly drawing strength from the opportunities created by their mistakes. They wrestle the harsh spotlight from sideline commentators, critically examine their shortcomings, and expose their failures as well as the process of healing and growth for all to see. Let's look at how you can embrace risk, accountability, and community to rebound from mistakes with more strength and trust than ever before.

Stop looking for certainty and embrace the risk

The COVID-19 outbreak of 2020 offers object lessons in seizing opportunity from the ruin of hesitation and cowardice. Despite warnings from foreign governments and domestic public health officials, the Trump White House failed to offer clear communication, direction, or leadership about the mounting threat of the novel coronavirus through January and February 2020. As state and local communities started to report community spread, the federal government offered inconsistent guidance, frequently walking back details, and failing to empathize with those affected by the pandemic.

By March 15, governors in Washington, California, New York, and Massachusetts had closed schools, bars, and restaurants. They recommended or required citizens to shelter in place and maintain social distancing. Malls, playgrounds, and gyms closed. But in Florida, beaches remained open, luring an enthusiastic spring break crowd. The state's commitment to tourism underscored the inadequate understanding of the threat and patchwork local responses led by mixed messaging from the White House.

Rather than following the ample lessons of other countries, the White House didn't call for social distancing or require sheltering in place. Shirking more concrete mandates favored by many states, on March 16 the president said that people should "avoid gathering in groups of more than 10" and "should stay away from bars, restaurants, and food courts, and to not travel if possible," but avoided anything firmer.[1]

In the San Francisco Bay Area, another response played out. On February 28, Dr. Sara Cody, director of Santa Clara County's Public Health Department, stood behind the mic at a press conference. She offered concrete advice about the known transmission vectors of COVID-19: "Today, start working on not touching your face—because one main way viruses spread is when you touch your own mouth, nose, or eyes."[2] Then she lifted a finger to her mouth, licked it, and turned the page in her notes. The gaffe went viral as people mocked Dr. Cody—but that human foible drew attention to the challenge facing everyone.

Dr. Cody was a month into formulating Santa Clara County's coronavirus response, which has since proven to be a successful and model example of action and communication. On January 31, the White House announced a ban on foreign nationals who had visited China in the past two weeks, exempting foreign nationals with immediate family in the US.[3] But that move was too little, too late—and misdirected. The problem wasn't the virus coming from China. As Dr. Cody explained in her January 31 press conference, the virus was already here.[4] Santa Clara County, spanning Palo Alto to

Gilroy, had a positive confirmation of the Bay Area's first case of coronavirus. Speaking in clear terms and sharing evolving information about methods of transmission, she delivered concise, actionable information to an anxious audience.

Trust in public leadership demands that balance of vulnerability and certainty. Act slowly in an effort to wait for more information, and you risk public health and lose the sense of urgency. Act too quickly, and you risk making mistakes or causing a panic. Act too gently so as not ruffle feathers or stoke fear, and you risk undermining the audience's ability to take matters seriously. Act too severely, and you risk public ridicule. Without direction on a federal-level response, Dr. Cody acted with courage and rose to the dual challenge of global pandemic and federal pandemonium.

She began making the tough calls. She banned festivals, closed schools, and required people to work from home. Public gatherings were severely limited. She reached out to a team of legal and public health colleagues to ensure the collective wisdom focused on the effort.

On March 16, Dr. Cody led a team including colleagues across seven counties to mandate the country's first shelter-in-place order;[5] several days later, Governor Gavin Newsom expanded the mandate to the entire state.[6]

"You have to really know your partners and you have to trust them and they have to trust you," Dr. Cody said in an interview with *The Mercury News*.[7] "And it can't move fast unless you have that high level of trust. And we have that in our county. And I never realized how exceptional it was. But it turns out, it's pretty exceptional. And that's allowed us to be nimble and be honest and lead." Under pressure, siloed teams that lack leadership stumble and crumble. But by learning to communicate and build inter-departmental trust in an easy period, your team can act with speed and alignment in the face of crisis or decisions with increased risk.

"We needed to embrace the risk and do it," she said of acting decisively about social distancing, business closures, and shelter-in-place restrictions. Rather than shirking the responsibility, her bold actions started the process of flattening the curve, delaying the outbreak's impact on the public health system. Bold actions belied her reasoned, thoughtful process, as made evident in the calm, clear voice of Bay Area public health. Other politicians have berated communities for flouting shelter-in-place orders. Trump and his White House subordinates have argued openly with reporters and evaded concrete details.

Dr. Cody approached press conferences and public communication with a different tone, offering consistency, actionable detail, and approachable empathy—for healthcare workers, patients, caregivers, small business owners, and parents. "I was thinking about the people who live in our county," she told *The Mercury News*, "the people that run small business, the people who are living right on the edge and how what I was doing was going to profoundly impact them personally and professionally." Empathy, not bluster or platitudes, won her trust and respect. Enough for people to listen and for the Bay Area to start to flatten the curve.

In an evolving story demanding swift communication, it's tempting to wait until details and direction are concrete, final, and beyond reproach. That's safe. But public health doesn't offer that certainty, safety, and distance. Leadership means

drawing on experience to brave risk in the face of vulnerability, and cultivating a conversation that allows for mistakes
and unknowns.

April Starr's Cancer Worksheets offer some of that space
for unknowns. For all its process, modern medicine doesn't
always have all the answers—for patients, or for their doctors.
"When you're diagnosed, you're immediately not empowered,"
she explains. "All your power is taken away from you. It's hard
to get a cancer diagnosis without immediately thinking about
death. You're thinking, 'I don't know what to do, I don't know
how to control this thing.' The people around you that you've
never met, you've never worked with them; you've probably
never seen an oncologist before, and you don't know what to
expect." The nature of oncology means that physicians may
not always know what to expect either—but in openly discussing those "known unknowns" with patients and their families,
they can start to build trust.

Describing gaps in knowledge or admitting that they don't
yet have all the answers is foreign to many practitioners.
Their vulnerability can help patients trust the process and
allow them to extend grace to their care team. "It's like project planning," says April. "You don't always know where it's
going to go, but you can still establish milestones. Doctors
often do that, but they don't always share it with the patient."
The worksheets facilitate the simple act of sharing the milestones so everyone has the same information and feels like
they can participate in the decision-making process with
confidence—a simple but rare level of engagement.

Embrace accountability to empathize with your audience

Framing a conversation around unknowns lays the ground-work for sustaining trust in the aftermath of mistakes as well. The Controlled Risk Insurance Company (CRICO) is the insurance program for all Harvard medical institu-tions. It provides medical malpractice insurance for nearly 30 hospitals, 14,000 physicians, and 100,000 clinicians and employees. For more than 15 years, CRICO has led a cultural shift in how doctors address medical errors. Rather than suggesting they deny responsibility, CRICO encourages clini-cians to "undertake uncomfortable conversations not simply to avoid lawsuits, but because it's the right thing to do."[8] The organization studied outcomes from medical errors and dis-covered that, whether in cases of negligence or in the standard of care, when healthcare providers accept responsibility and apologize both clinician and patient can move forward with greater satisfaction and without protracted litigation.

"We found that the surgeons did the best in the area of explaining the medical facts of the event," explained Dr. Thomas Gallagher in the "Surgeons and Error Disclosure" episode of CRICO's *Patient Safety Updates* podcast.[9] Galla-gher, an associate professor of medicine, medical history, and ethics at the University of Washington, co-authored a study published in the November 2005 issue of *Surgery*.[10] "But they struggled in other areas," he said on the podcast. "For instance, the surgeons had difficulty taking responsibility for the event, apologizing for the event, and very few of the surgeons said anything to the patients about how recurrences of the error would be prevented. And these are all areas and types of information that patients have told us in previous studies really matters to them."

Taking responsibility, apologizing, and describing steps for changing behavior all demand practice in vulnerability—but that practice is a skill that people can learn, and organizations can operationalize. Far from being a nuanced marketing technique, vulnerability is a return to basic communication skills.

We are most vulnerable when we center ourselves in owning the problem, even if all the information hasn't come in yet. In a case of medical negligence or human error, it's as basic as speaking in the first person and simple language. *I did this. I'm sorry.* What doesn't work and erodes trust? *This happened. We extend our sympathies.* Start with empathy for the patient that validates their feelings. "Physicians frequently feel empathetic for a patient," says Dr. Wendy Levinson,[11] one of Dr. Gallagher's co-authors, who also offered her comments on the CRICO podcast. Levinson is a researcher in physician-patient communication and chair of medicine at the University of Toronto. "They see a patient feeling sad, but how does the patient know the doctor feels empathic unless the doctor says something?" Say something simple and concrete. *I know this must be overwhelming. I can imagine how painful this must be.* We can express concern and hold space for an uncomfortable conversation, especially if that's best for both the person who's been hurt and the improvement of our own work and practice.

Communicate at the speed of change—and screwups

Responding to failures with promises to improve doesn't mean you should revel in some perverse and pollyannaish silver lining, but smart organizations see the opportunity to grow that comes from mistakes.

Rapid change and the learning that comes with it is the common story of brands on Kickstarter, the home of prototyping in public and revealing growth, warts and all. The Fidget Cube, a palm-sized vinyl desk toy, is a product of that process. The cube features a rocker switch, glide wheel, clicky buttons, rolling gears, and rotating dial—a handheld delight for people who struggle to focus, students with ADHD, or anyone with nervous energy. Antsy Labs launched the campaign for the Fidget Cube in the summer of 2016, promising shipment in time for Christmas. In the interim, the company partnered with customers to develop the color palette, finalized supplier contracts, began production, and managed quality control. Matthew and Mark McLachlan, the brothers who designed the Fidget Cube and who helm Antsy Labs, launched the crowdfunding campaign with this perspective: "This isn't our first rodeo. We've brought several Kickstarter projects to life in the past, and have learned from our experiences. While we have been relentlessly concerned with the details throughout designing, prototyping, and planning for production, there is always the chance that pesky Murphy guy may make an entrance with that law of his. In the event that things don't go as planned, whether it's a delay in the manufacturing timeline, shipping date, or something else, we promise to communicate honestly with you and work around the clock until we correct the issue."[12] That promise proved prescient.

On December 7, 2016, Antsy Labs posted a GIF-adorned update to the campaign's backers: the product would begin shipping in less than 10 days, by the end of the following week! "However, depending on ship times, where you're located, and your backer number, your reward may ship in December but have a delivery date after the 25th,"[13] they warned. Maybe rethink that Christmas present. For backers who'd hoped to use Fidget Cube as a stocking stuffer, the company offered "some downloadables that you'll be able to give in the meantime." The message may have been disappointing, but it was clear and early enough to allow people time to revise their gift plans.

The message also revealed challenges in the process. As they geared up manufacturing, Antsy Labs was also working to counter competitors, as knockoff and counterfeit products popped up on eBay that often suffered from nonfunctioning components or subpar materials. They also struggled to keep up with backer input, a vital feature of Kickstarter campaigns. Fidget Cube had an exceptionally active backer community, with more than 150,000 people pledging more than $6 million to bring the product to life—far more than the company anticipated, or had prepared to support.

"Due to the incredible workload leading up to shipping, we have unfortunately not been able to be present in the comments," they explained in their December 7 update. "Our team is now growing to include an Antsy Labs Scientist. This individual will browse the comments and weigh in when they're able to, and will be identifiable by the highlighted label next to their profile name. Any questions that may come up in the comments can be addressed to them. We hope that this will further increase the availability of information coming directly from the Antsy Labs team moving forward." When communication lapsed, the company swiftly apologized to the community, took responsibility, and offered a solution to prevent the problem from occurring again. While in a far less serious and consequential context, Antsy Labs followed the same template as CRICO offers physicians.

While campaigns on Kickstarter often exemplify this kind of risk-taking and accountability, your organization can operationalize vulnerability too. Set clear expectations for the frequency of communication with stakeholders and/or collaborators—on Kickstarter, they are one and the same. Develop a governance plan or contract that specifies the frequency, format, and detail of communication when things go wrong. In both internal and external projects, they often do: products are delayed, timelines slip, manufacturers change factories. By designing templates for difficult updates and editorial language to communicate what happened, by whom, and what will be done to resolve the issue, your team doesn't need to hide in shame. Instead, you can pick yourselves up and move forward openly, and bring your colleagues, prospective customers, or community along with you.

That's what Antsy Labs needed to do, repeatedly.

On January 4, 2017, the company said that shipping had finally begun, far later than they'd originally planned, in part due to quality control issues, and in part due to much higher volume than they'd anticipated. "Although we wished we could have shipped these to you back in October when our project ended, we had to (and continue to) make sure Fidget Cube was a finished product that met our incredibly high standards," they wrote.[14] However, by January 26, they still hadn't shipped all of the products promised in December.[15]

"A majority of December rewards have been shipped out to backers and by next week we will be at about 80% of December orders shipped. As you know, we are shipping as we get inventory," the company wrote. "Had we known that there would be delays in shipments and deliveries of some of your rewards, we would have told you from the very start. It has always been our goal to deliver as soon as possible, and as you all know by now [...] we did not want to compromise the quality of Fidget Cube to push shipments out the door faster. There are many moving pieces to a project of this magnitude, and while we would love to have the ability to control 100% of these pieces, the fact of the matter is that there are unfortunately processes that take time." Though there's a temptation to stop communicating when news is bad, or to over-promise and hope for the best, Antsy Labs aimed to be clear, communicate with detail, and ask for their customers' understanding.

The community response was mixed, in part because Antsy Labs broke a cardinal rule of communication: actions speak louder than words. Backers reported getting the same message, copied in response to every email: "We're expecting some large shipments to our warehouses within the next week which should allow us to fulfill all remaining orders. While we don't have an exact date that your specific order will ship out, we will send a shipping notification as soon as your package is on its way!" Some recipients were infuriated by the unchanging repetition. Others offered more generous comments. "I've seen a lot worse communication, and a lot worse fulfillment," wrote one backer. "I know some people don't bother understanding what they're signing up for when they back a Kickstarter, and you've got a pretty tough backer base given this is designed to help with anxiety. Thanks for keeping us updated—yes, I'm anxious to get mine, but I'm not going to panic for another month or so."

Another month put the campaign into March.

Antsy Labs maintained a consistent communication schedule, relaying information from their manufacturing partners about every two weeks. However, they admitted to problems: fielding 2,000 incoming emails a day on top of managing shipments to the initial 100,000 backers got in the way of responsive communication. "We've heard backers in the Fidget Family express agitation over slower than usual response times for emails," Antsy Labs posted in an update.[16] "In the last week, we have added two additional customer service members and as of this weekend will have a team of six more." Backers continued to complain, citing slow communication on a campaign that now seemed suspicious, especially as knockoffs hit the market. However, as Fidget Cubes reached more and more of the original backers, comments grew more positive, saying it was worth the wait. The company reached out to ensure that all backers completed their orders by providing a mailing address and color preference. By April 2017, Antsy Labs announced all original and complete backer orders had been fulfilled. They launched a new campaign the following January.

In the interim, the company had the chance to breathe and learn from their mistakes. Most problems revolved around communication. "When we launched Fidget Cube, we had a goal of $15,000. We had certainly hoped for more than that, but had not remotely expected or planned for what happened, which was a blessing and unfortunately a bit of a curse," the McLachlan brothers shared in an update.[17] Crowdfunding more than 400 times that amount brought nightmares of scale in manufacturing, fulfillment, and communication. "When we launched Fidget Cube, we had every intention of personally replying to most comments on the page and having very consistent updates," wrote the founders. "However, as the project went on and the community grew exponentially, we found ourselves struggling to stay afloat on a day-to-day basis. We believe this is in large part due to the sudden need we faced to scale so rapidly. We've had many days where we were getting an average of two emails a minute. What we eventually ended up doing is using a service to help with this workload. In the future, we will most likely be using an outside group to handle our PR and customer service as it's an extremely important aspect of any business, let alone a company that is using crowdfunding." That awareness came too late for customers who were investing in an idea and wanted the engagement of smaller campaigns, though "superbackers" familiar with crowdfunding continued to write favorable comments about the product. Vulnerable communication endeared most of their backers to the company and underscored their investment in the process. Greater awareness helped Antsy Labs evolve as a company that now produces and licenses a range of popular products, many of which have launched through Kickstarter.

The experiences of Antsy Labs offer powerful lessons for anyone: as things go wrong, communicate early and often. Speak in the first person to explain what your organization did and where things went off the rails. Offer the most accurate and complete detail possible, even if it needs to be revised later. When you do need to revise estimates and timelines, go back to the template: apologize, explain what new thing happened, and explain what you'll do so this *new* problem doesn't happen again. Eventually, we all grow up, and hope to get more things right; that process of maturing applies to startups, public figures, and new product lines as well.

Draw community close to build loyalty—and a better product

TED offers another example of vulnerability, listening, and engaging thoughtfully with your community to rebound from problems with grace. Founded as an annual conference of a few hundred big thinkers in "technology, entertainment, and design," TED now comprises the much-loved TED.com platform and a licensing model that extends the brand and its imprimatur to thousands of local events and a global audience. The TED community is a source of strength, accountability, and oversight to the organization. The idea of "community" has evolved from big thinkers and loyal fans to now encompass critics and commentators as well. Headline-grabbing missteps caused the TED organization to acknowledge and engage their community with vulnerability and humility, a position that wasn't always part of the brand. As they embraced a broader understanding of their audience, TED listened and learned from critics who expected the organization to hold itself to a higher standard in quality and publishing, even as it extended its brand and platform to independent events. Though at times these critics scorned the organization for advancing ideas without peer oversight, they still paid attention and could offer guidance to help TED improve.

"People come to TED for insight, surprise, knowledge they don't have yet," says Emily McManus, founding managing editor of TED.com. "For TED to seem smart and authoritative helps to build their trust." The website conveys those qualities through the talks it elevates, cultivating content from both the main conference and the top 1% of talks at regional events, and the copy that frames the talks. "When we conduct user interviews and ask people what talks seem most authoritative, we learn that if the blurb is a little longer, people seem to trust it more. Then we're careful not to use a lot of long words in the description so the text doesn't look dense," she says. "There's a lot of white space so you can read it quickly." This design choice signals respect for the audience and empowers them to choose where to direct their attention, rather than steering their attention to marquee content. The editorial team made other decisions that ceded control to the audience. "When we first launched, we privileged speaker name over topic," Emily says. "But in our first major redesign in 2013, we found the name isn't nearly as interesting as the topic. Part of our mission is to put up talks from people who aren't very famous." TED promises *ideas* worth spreading, not personalities in search of visibility. "In 2017, we had talks by the Pope and Monica Lewinsky—but if you take them out, the top talk from the 2017 conference was from Anil Seth, talking about our consciousness," says Emily. "The guy you never heard of is doing amazing research and earned 4 million views in the first month." Those views were driven by a design that promoted a headline and topic, not the speaker name.

That approach allowed TED to use its platform to elevate ideas—but it also exposed the brand to risk. In 2009, TED launched TEDx, a program to support licensed, independent local TED-style events. The community and source of content grew through TEDx events, but they brought less oversight to the process of vetting ideas for quality. TED has since responded by rolling out content guidelines that address scientific credibility, peer review, and other markers.

For TED to "hold on loosely" to the content of licensed events, the stakes are high. Poor execution or minimal vetting can diminish brand value and undermine trust.

"At TEDx, speakers and talks aren't vetted by TED," Emily explains. At TEDxCharlotte 2010, Randy Powell delivered a talk titled "Vortex-Based Mathematics." The video went viral a year and a half later. Despite the initial applause, it was excoriated by scientists and media outlets, who saw Powell's claims of solving world hunger through a base 9 number system as completely empty. "Random word associations have long been a part of the TED approach, but it's called poetry, not science," Michael V. Copeland commented in *Wired*.[18] Writing in *The New Republic*, Evgeny Morozov decried TED as "no longer a responsible curator of 'ideas worth spreading.'"[19] Echoing CRICO's approach to accountability and apology,

TED took responsibility for quality control at regional events and jumped into the conversation to learn and discuss how to prevent the problem in the future.

"People take TED seriously, and obviously we'd been duped by someone and people wanted us to be responsible," Emily explains. "Powell believed in vortex math and presented it in an intoxicating mix of friendly, easy-to-understand language. It was compelling. You can't be mad at the people who put him on stage." But academics were angry and TED's broad audience was upset. So, she joined the conversation on *Slate*, Quora, NPR, CNN, and dozens of other media outlets. Rather than engage in PR spin, Emily sought to discuss the issue and cultivate a solution.

"By communicating publicly and person-to-person, TED achieved two things. One was to signal that it was paying attention to people's concerns. But more strategically, TED learned about a systemic problem that demanded a broad solution," wrote Nilofer Merchant in *Harvard Business Review*.[20] By transparently discussing the problem with community-supported content, TED also sought to socialize the effort to fix it. In an open conversation with critics, they acknowledged weaknesses, drew out constructive feedback, and brainstormed with an equally passionate audience. Their vulnerability brought the audience closer to strengthen the brand, as well as its licensed events and content.

The product and process behind it reflects stronger governance. New content guidelines and new science standards specify the kind of content allowed on many TEDx stages. Moreover, the organization doesn't shy away from addressing

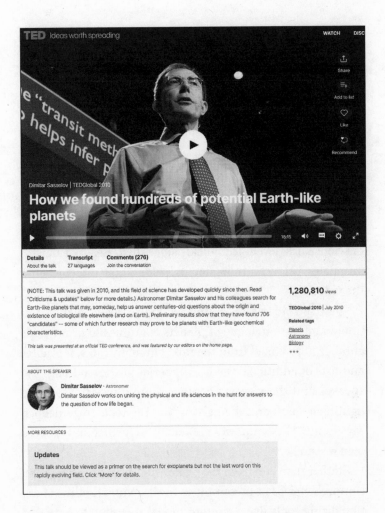

FIGURE 9.1 The note and update on Dimitar Sasselov's TED talk put it in context of evolving science, not to diminish its value but to empower anyone who might reference it with information worth spreading.

talks that may become outdated or irrelevant in the face of newer science. TED.com developed new content types and messaging to direct viewers to more recent talks as well as an editorial review process to add commentary on older talks or talks that may be considered partisan.

"Astronomer Dimitar Sasselov spoke when we were just starting to get back the data on Earth-like planets," Emily explains. "He shared that we'd discovered hundreds of exoplanets—but that was 10 years ago." Ongoing research has revealed thousands of exoplanets, and the number continues to grow. "NOTE: This talk was given in 2010, and this field of science has developed quickly since then. Read 'Criticisms & updates' below for more details," adds a note directly below the video.[21]

"New and old telescopes unveil hundreds of exoplanets routinely, and the catalogue of planets continues to grow," adds another note linked from the talk. On many talks, footnotes and lists of additional reading material further aid both the speaker and the viewer. "Footnotes are a way to say we're lighting a spark and then giving you the tools to go deeper," says Emily. They empower viewers to go further and do their own research.

Rather than run from the responsibility to be current and comprehensive, TED.com turns toward vulnerability, operationalizing tools like a content model to annotate outdated content and responsibly curate talks, even those from 10 years ago. "If you're a science teacher, we're not going to make you feel silly for watching it, but we're going to make sure you understand the context around it," notes Emily. That attention to responsibility and acknowledgment of vulnerabilities is the bedrock for trust, even in one of the most trusted publishing brands.

Evolve in public to hold yourself accountable

Just as TED seeks to democratize access to information, American clothing retailer Old Navy seeks to democratize access to fashion. Launching in 1994 with a goal of making fashionable clothing at a broadly accessible price point, they fit into Gap Inc.'s mandate for "inclusion by design"[22] by actively recruiting a diverse workforce at all levels of the company, designing for extended sizes and a universal fit on the majority of products, seeking out diverse suppliers, and reporting openly on progress toward their goals in those areas. "To understand where we have room to improve, we're measuring our progress," the company says to frame its annual sustainability report.[23] It focuses on accountability, not just accomplishment.

As you saw with Penzeys, when companies make their passions public they can make a wonderful impact, but risk scorn, reprisal, and financial loss. They also run another risk: by putting a stake in the ground, it's doubly raw and embarrassing when they miss the mark and the public catches them deviating from those values. Old Navy expressed their commitment to racial diversity and inclusion and eventually faced this issue. They chose to improve just as transparently and vulnerably as they began, by exposing their work in progress, renewing a commitment to anti-discrimination practices, and communicating that commitment in accessible language and visible partnerships.

In 2019, Old Navy was getting ready to celebrate the brand's 25th anniversary. Their original CEO was a woman of color, and they were proud that their most recent CEO was a woman of color as well. To mark the occasion, they announced a new partnership and significant donation to Open to All, a nationwide coalition of businesses and non-profits that pledge to support nondiscrimination efforts and welcome everyone through corporate policy, business operations, ongoing training, visible badging, and vocal support. The organization seeks out members who embody the work and aren't just seeking to put the Open to All sticker on a window to cover up a questionable history.

The anniversary celebrations and partnership with Open to All came a year after an incident that ran counter to the company's work in anti-bias advocacy and inclusion. James Conley, a 29-year-old Black man, accused staff and management at an Old Navy in Des Moines, Iowa, of racial profiling after they suggested he was attempting to shoplift the coat he was wearing. They asked him to take it off so that they could scan it. At his insistence, they eventually reviewed security camera footage and saw that he'd been wearing the coat when he came in. He left with his coat, but without an apology for how they'd treated him. Local media quickly picked up the story.

At the corporate level, Old Navy reacted decisively. A senior executive apologized on behalf of the company and fired the employees who were involved while conducting a broader investigation and providing frequent updates to the media.

"What's amazing is, even though this incident happened, Old Navy acted quickly," explains Calla Rongerude, the campaign director of Open to All. Old Navy and Gap Inc. are in the campaign's Leadership Circle. This incident exposed the systemic nature of racism and the challenge that even more socially minded organizations face to drive corporate policy into everyday customer interactions.

"Retailers know that you can express your values and offer corporate anti-racism training but you can't control everyone you employ," Calla says. Much like TED discovered in its licensed events, and Antsy Labs discovered in its supply chain, it's challenging to design for control—but communication coupled with decisive action can fill the gaps that undermine trust. "We can never have 100% confidence that people will always be treated with the respect they deserve. The companies we work with understand that; they respond by saying the right thing, doing the right thing, and taking responsibility that it happened in their store—and that it's a problem in our culture."

Saying the right thing means apologizing, restating the organization's values, and sharing that the company is investigating what happened. "We encourage people to apologize— bottom line, someone left your store and felt hurt. You expend no capital to acknowledge that. Only good will can be gained," explains Calla. "Our current political climate doesn't always allow us to listen to another person and validate their experiences. We have a culture where it's so easy to dismiss each other—but the most important thing is for a company to make sure their customer is seen, heard, and validated. At the same time, they can investigate and get the facts." While that investigation can expose personnel issues that result in private termination, companies can continue to speak openly about their culture, values, and how they're working to bring local actions in line with their values.

Old Navy committed to further ongoing anti-racism training and continued to address what had happened, stating in a Facebook post, "The situation was a violation of our policies and values, and we apologize to both Mr. Conley and to those we've disappointed. All of our customers deserve to be treated with respect. [...] We take this matter—and every conversation around equality—very seriously. Old Navy is committed to ensuring that our stores are an environment where everyone feels welcome."[24] Calla acknowledges their ongoing work and Old Navy's commitment to their partnership. "Our sticker won't make a problematic history go away," she says. "Instead, Old Navy wrestled the big questions and consulted with us to be agents of change in this area. Being welcoming is a big part of the Old Navy brand; they want customers to know they will be respected when they come in, so they partnered with us because that's a value they want to stand behind."

Old Navy offers a lesson in embracing opportunities to improve, by shouldering responsibility to respond in a system that otherwise perpetuates racism. We grow stronger—in public health, in medical practice, in product design, and in anti-bias efforts of social justice—by building trust. But when we embrace vulnerability, with its tough conversations and public apologies, we commit to prototype in public, without artifice or spin. The brand is naked—and that moment puts faith and trust in the audience just as must as it helps build their trust in us. Strong organizations embrace the opportunity to build trust at their most vulnerable moments. Paradoxically, those moments can be pivotal and empowering.

Zoom found itself in the middle of a most vulnerable moment. If luck is where preparation meets opportunity, the remote conferencing platform is lucky. In 2019, they rolled out a robust phone version. They also implemented a range of new features, including advanced virtual backgrounds and virtual waiting rooms to hold people waiting for a host to let them join a meeting, features that would prove valuable in unanticipated ways. Then as businesses and municipalities responded to COVID-19 by mandating people work from home and schools embraced remote learning, usage of Zoom exploded. Ninety thousand schools across 20 countries jumped on the platform. Families connected for birthday celebrations, holiday meals, and virtual visits and friends met online for happy hours and viewing parties. In December 2019, before the virus reached pandemic proportions, Zoom counted no more than 10 million daily meeting participants, most of whom were business customers. By March 2020, the platform saw daily usage exceed 200 million participants—families, friends, preschool teachers, university professors, professional speakers, and enterprise business teams included.

Zoom rose to the occasion to support the increase in number and types of users—but the growth wasn't without enormous challenges that exposed weaknesses in the platform. On April 1, 2020, Zoom CEO Eric Yuan discussed the problems and plans to address them in a powerful post on the Zoom blog.[25] It's a case study in timely, specific, and transparent communication in the wake of problems, and a testament to growing through the opportunity they present.

"Usage of Zoom ballooned overnight—far surpassing what we expected when we first announced our desire to help in late February," he wrote. The good problem to have—so many new users!—quickly created bad problems for the support team and attracted bad actors to the platform. Trolls targeted public meetings by screen sharing and "zoombombing" unwitting participants with pornography, racist screeds, and anti-Semitic attacks.[26]

"We recognize we have fallen short of the community's—and our own—privacy and security expectations," Yuan continued. "For that, I am deeply sorry, and I want to share what we are doing about it." While Yuan described the team's goals and efforts in the plural to share the credit, he used the first-person singular to apologize. The CEO alone shouldered the responsibility.

The post moved into specific technical details—not to baffle readers, but to empower them with a better understanding of the landscape, challenges, and roadmap.

"First, some background: our platform was built primarily for enterprise customers—large institutions with full IT support," Yuan wrote. "Thousands of enterprises around the world have done exhaustive security reviews of our user, network, and data center layers and confidently selected Zoom for complete deployment." He reminded readers that Zoom is robust and tested—though not tested for quite this situation.

"We did not design the product with the foresight that, in a matter of weeks, every person in the world would suddenly be working, studying, and socializing from home," he continued. "We now have a much broader set of users who are utilizing our product in a myriad of unexpected ways, presenting us with challenges we did not anticipate when the platform was conceived. These new, mostly consumer-use cases have helped us uncover unforeseen issues with our platform." Here, Yuan pivots to make a "you're using it wrong!" problem into an opportunity. That's not spin; it's smart leadership. He moves on to credit the community: "Dedicated journalists and security researchers have also helped to identify pre-existing ones. We appreciate the scrutiny and questions we have been getting—about how the service works, about our infrastructure and capacity, and about our privacy and security policies. These are the questions that will make Zoom better, both as a company and for all its users."

Finally, he laid out a timeline for what Zoom will do. Number one? "Enacting a feature freeze and shifting all our engineering resources to focus on our biggest trust, safety, and privacy issues." By the following week, Zoom made those virtual waiting rooms and meeting passwords the default for all new meetings. Users soon realized that "fun" features like virtual backgrounds offered privacy benefits by hiding the details of home life for students and colleagues suddenly forced to reveal the physical surroundings of their home office.

Yuan closed by explaining how the community—consumers, businesses, schools, and media—can hold him accountable. He promised to conduct weekly webinars about Zoom's privacy updates, publish a transparency report, and submit to third-party audits. His response to Zoom's problems was swift, specific, transparent, and vulnerable—making this a powerful case study in how to earn trust while confronting trouble.

Smart organizations learn to operationalize authenticity and vulnerability as more than mere buzzwords when faced with a crisis, production delays, or technical difficulties. Consider darker moments that call upon your bravery, when design must outthink cynicism. When confronting the risks of prototyping in public and facing criticism, transform vulnerability from a point of weakness into a source of courage— and leadership.

The Bay Area's coronavirus response team faced risk and from the top down acted courageously. The San Francisco Digital Services team published web content at a surprising rate and with a high level of accuracy because content creators were free to move forward in the framework of content strategy and familiar style guidelines. The communication demands were too pressing to wait for certainty or layers of legal approval, so people had to trust the system, their tools, and each other. At Zoom, the team followed a culture of accountability, collaboration, and transparency, modeled by the CEO.

If your organization wrangles matters of equal importance— or far less—can you build systems to operationalize and support vulnerability and risk? Do you follow in the model of Antsy Labs, and aim to communicate at the speed of change? Do your audience one better: bring them close by sharing more of the underlying details and factors that drive bad news, in the hope of fostering their understanding and loyalty. It's that power of community that builds a stronger company and experience, as TED knows so well. Do you give your community the respect necessary to earn their trust? Embrace the risk to grow, prototype in public, and model growth. As Old Navy demonstrates, improving our companies and teams is the thing that we can do, the change we can most immediately effect, to improve our society as a whole. Like a bone healing after a break, you can grow a bit stronger at the point of previous weakness, modeling a process of improvement and self-awareness won not through the sheen of success, but through the sweat and grit of vulnerability, resilience, and renewal. Naked and vulnerable, you can find strength to empower your brand and audiences at the same time.

CHAPTER 10

Vision for the future

Cynicism is nothing but intellectual cowardice.
HENRY ROLLINS *Provoked* [1]

WHEN YOU ask your readers, users, customers, or clients to trust your brand, there's an implicit bargain in the works. You ask them to trust you and, in return, you commit to being trustworthy. You commit to do what you say, align your actions with your values, and hold yourself accountable when you slip up. You tell your audiences to hold you accountable, too. Those commitments demand that courage triumphs over cowardice.

Another agreement underpins your commitment to being trustworthy: to get trust, you need to give trust. And this isn't a game of counting to three and then speaking at the same time; you have to go first. In asking your audience to trust you, you have to be willing to trust them—with yourself. With who you are, the unique perspective of your brand. With your brand's passions and focus. And with all the ways you're screwing up, learning, and growing. What could go wrong?

Can you count on them getting your jokes and understanding your lingo?

Will they mock what makes you different?

Do they care enough to stick with your company as it evolves?

Will they pick at you and kick you for sharing your weaknesses?

Will they sneer if you strip off the varnish and let big ideas shine through simple words?

Does their interest mirror your enthusiasm, or will they get bored after too many words?

Will they suspect simple words, after predatory business and bureaucracy have honed their skepticism?

If you help people get smarter, will they still need your organization?

What if they can't relate to your experience or the way your brand bids for their attention?

Do they even care to share in the issues that drive your company?

Do they want to get involved in helping you evolve?

Do they even care about making things better?

Yes, to all of that—even the bad stuff. You can trust your audience to be human, and we humans contain multitudes. We are critical, skeptical, and broken by bureaucracy. But people are also endlessly hopeful—and as marketers, designers, and writers, we have the challenge of affirming their hope amid a world hell-bent on trampling it. Consider the landscape and how we got to a moment where expertise is both invaluable and under suspicion.

Amid terrifying, confusing times, we see endless examples of why we should turn away from the false words and intentional obfuscation of television pundits and political leaders. And over the past decade, old arbiters of truth and so-called experts lost their appeal. There is no Walter Cronkite to offer a definitive perspective on the day's events. Instead, people turned to friends and to reviews from "people just like you" to get a bead on the news, pick a restaurant, or plan a vacation—but right when we noticed our filter bubbles, they began to burst. We learned hotels gamed their reviews and algorithms and bad actors drove popular stories in our newsfeeds. Skeptical of outside sources, many people turned inward for the truth. Away from scientific scrutiny and more inclusive social policy, it's easy to find comfort in familiar beliefs. What *feels* right can be more attractive than what *is* right.

This self-fulfilling, egocentric wisdom gains strength on the fuel of disdain for rigorous intellectualism. Today, only 35% of Americans say they have "a great deal of confidence" in scientists to act in the public interest.[2] If we can't trust the motivations of scientists, can we trust the information and warnings they publish? A Yale study revealed that 43% of Americans dismiss the role of humans in climate change—if they believe in it at all.[3] But scorn masks something far simpler: cynicism. Cynics look at the world as it is and say it's worse. They pull back, too fearful to engage in improving it. But most people are not so devoid of opinions and criticism as to completely give up. Even people who pretend to be jaded, indifferent, or apathetic still jump in when engaged directly.

We all have opinions.

Participation is evidence of something else at work: not cynicism, but hope.

Even after losing faith in experts and turning inward for truth, we remain hopeful—and curious. Most people want to learn and do better and seek direction from the institutions around them. We want to be better and we want our world to be better. Those 35% of Americans who say they feel quite confident scientists generally act in the public interest? That number is up from just 21% in 2016. In comparison to confidence in the motivations of the military, religious leaders, business leaders, and elected officials, scientists are the only group whose public perception has consistently improved. Has our need for experts to be "the grown-ups in the room" increased in inverse proportion to mounting revelations of ethical problems in those other groups? Or have our expectations of transparency increased, stoked by the efforts of the #TimesUp campaign, visibility of #MeToo, persistence of the Consumer Financial Protection Bureau, and scrutiny of accountability watchdogs like Sleeping Giants and Grab Your Wallet?[4] The reason matters less than the result: people hope to improve, and we expect the institutions around us to hold themselves accountable to improvement too.

More transparent, trustworthy institutions grow by improving and by helping the people around them improve too. The evidence is in these pages: organizations earn trust and rebuild people's trust in themselves by communicating through a consistent voice, the right volume to enable confident decisions, and vulnerability to critical feedback. Taken separately, those points are guidelines for good content and user-centered design. Applied together, they can elevate your organization to lead and foster trust.

With its easy-to-use interface and broad suite of services, Mailchimp consistently earns applause and an expanding user base. Among both critics and clients, it also earns trust. Small business owners count on its familiar voice, unique enough to stand out in a more humdrum marketplace and scrappy enough to communicate a creative, entrepreneurial sensibility. But while the brand is sacred, the voice is not. They're no longer the small business serving small businesses. As the company has grown over time, its voice has matured to better reflect the perspective of a maturing audience. It's still clearly Mailchimp—accessible, friendly—but now combines a direct tone and less fussy imagery to be more approachable to new users who may not be as familiar with the brand's history and inside jokes.

To support a wide range of services and wider range of business customers, Mailchimp offers support in many different ways. "You can look through guides, Knowledge Base (KB) articles, and tutorials for information. Mailchimp offers help sections for some of its new features like automation. You'll also find helpful videos on topics like 'Create an Automated Email,'" wrote Molly McLaughlin in a review for *PCMag*.[5] While it offers myriad content types, Mailchimp strikes a balance by offering less volume within the content itself. Pages begin with a concise "before you start" list and organize content under easy-to-scan headings and anchor links so the help is supportive, never overwhelming.

And the brand remains vulnerable, humbling itself to feedback and offering transparency to its practices. In 2019, Mailchimp published their first transparency report.[6] As other companies were castigated for complying with government requests for their users' personal information, Mailchimp proactively disclosed how it balanced its clients' right to privacy and compliance with the law. Plain language, definitions, and simple charts made the information accessible and clear. At times, Mailchimp's attention to client privacy exposes the company to criticism. In 2019, they attracted attention for dissolving a partnership with ecommerce platform Shopify.[7] The platform required customer data that breached Mailchimp customer privacy terms, per Mailchimp's statement. Some users were upset; the change required them to rework backend processes to maintain the integration. Mailchimp was open and detailed in explaining its decision but sympathetic to customers' concerns. It responded by publicizing workarounds, offering additional technical support, and elevating new solutions. Thoughtful support and hard business decisions coexist at mature organizations—and, with clear communication, can engender greater trust.

At Mailchimp, voice, volume, and vulnerability combine to build trust in the company and empower millions of small businesses at the same time. In their commitment to being trustworthy, Mailchimp is a partner in their users' success— and in the hope and dreams of all small businesses. They validate that hope with tools, services, and support to instill confidence in customers that they can realize their dreams, and that Mailchimp will help. By paying attention to voice, volume, and vulnerability, they maintain the trust of a broader audience and empower them to serve even more end users than ever before.

TED makes a similar commitment: by paying attention to voice, volume, and vulnerability, they create a more welcoming future for big ideas and offer support to the many stages on which they can spread. They began by fostering conversation in the wake of criticism. Voice and volume aren't just what you say and how much you say, but also what you communicate by listening. TED engaged its fiercest critics by cultivating their ideas and then assertively listening. They neither sat back nor defensively countered, but instead engaged thoughtfully to learn, understand, and change. TED's posture and involvement is echoed by political representatives who embrace town halls with their constituents, hands-on CEOs who hold frequent open floor meetings, and user experience teams who conduct frequent generative research and focus groups with users. Feedback is a gift. The team at TED established common ground to foster it and humbled themselves enough to receive it. Prototyping in public is uncomfortable, especially for such a visible organization. But TED reaped the benefits: they trusted the community to guide growth and gained greater trust for creating a stronger product. They grew beyond a platform that elevates ideas worth spreading to a brand that can help viewers determine whether they're worth spreading. By holding themselves accountable to quality, the TED team developed tools to help the community of local events maintain quality too. The combination of voice, volume, and vulnerability empowered and increased trust in TED, TEDx, and the worldwide community of people who share the talks with friends. Now *better* ideas are spreading as a force for education, innovation, and conversation about some of the world's biggest problems.

The engaged language of TED and Mailchimp fits with champions of simplicity like NHS and patient educators like Crutchfield and Lovehoney: these brands make their privileged speech accessible to all, invest in the right level of detail to help people help themselves, and embrace their critics with honesty and self-awareness. We know that the economy of communities depends on the trust between businesses and consumers, governments, and citizens. By following these lessons, these organizations nurture that trust because they become smarter and they help their audiences become smarter. Trust thrives because they don't cave to cynicism, but instead rise courageously to answer the call for hope. Is affirming the hope of your audience the easy option? No. It's far easier to cave to a deceitful, divisive world, stoke craven cynicism, and give oxygen to our users' worst fears. Some politicians, news organizations, and brands know this path well.

Zoom took a different path. Amid the attacks of bad actors, issues with security and privacy, and an onslaught of new users, they could have come out swinging. People used the platform in ways the company never expected. Video conferencing novices were thoughtless about safeguarding their privacy. Trolls were malicious and unyielding.

CEO Eric Yuan could have laid blame on the feet of users, abusers, and even Zoom's own engineers. Instead, he accepted responsibility and validated users' concerns. He met his audience where they were in a tone that was serious and respectful. He affirmed their emotion and offered logic, with a detailed explanation and action plan. With vulnerability and humility, he took responsibility for bad experiences in the first-person singular, then shared credit for a solution in the first-person plural. Rather than castigate zoombombers and work his audience into a fury, he calmed them with purpose and planning, sharing how Zoom would make the platform more secure and teach users to better protect their privacy. In the weeks following his blog post, the team acted decisively to demonstrate progress. He answered the call for courage not with cynicism, but with hope.

Hope in the face of cynicism drives April Starr's design work. After being overwhelmed by the impenetrable jargon, barrage of resources, and litany of procedures, she designed the Cancer Worksheets to force physicians to step out from behind desks and laptops and meet their patients without the artifice of language. They gather around simple documents to unpack jargon, lay out an action plan, strip away conflicting and distracting details, and clarify their shared goals. The process pulls together language in the right voice, useful volume of detail, and vulnerability that humanizes patient and physician. By design, it increases patients' trust in their care team—but that benefit is almost ancillary. By empowering patients and their families, it helps them gain confidence in the new knowledge and courage in their convictions to do the right thing. An empowered patient can trust that they have all the information to make the best decisions in their own treatment. Doctors gain trust in their patients' decision-making abilities as well, key to bringing more respect into the doctor-patient relationship.

As a designer, April believed that the experience could be better for patients and their families. Her hope affirms their hope—there's got to be a better way. The Cancer Worksheets help patients have greater trust in themselves and their physicians because they validate that hope—and the belief that people are smart and want to be smarter. Zoom CEO Eric Yuan believes that his audience is smart and wants to be smarter, and customer advisors at Crutchfield, content designers at the FBI, and the team at the NHS all believe it, too. Yuan laid out a plan for a better platform that enables his audience to create a better world—that's a gamble on hope.

Remember, cynics look at the world as it is and say it's worse. But designers, writers, marketers, builders of brands and brainstorms—we look at the world as it is and say it can be better. If you are hopeful that it can be, work so that it will be.

So, do you respect that your audience is smart, and trust that they want to be smarter? That's what your audience wants. They aren't seeking your brand's authority; they're seeking their own self-improvement. They want to be more informed citizens, savvier consumers, better chefs, more worldly readers. If your organization can help them get there, you win their trust. By empowering people with information, building their confidence, and fostering their sense of trust, we can validate their hope—and rebuild society itself.

There's a spark we can't ignore. Of course, failures of leadership, wild inconsistencies, and deceptive practices of government, companies, and other institutions have left people overwhelmed, unmoored, and questioning their own gut instincts. But amid so many reasons to be cynical, hope still sparks inside us. You can fan that spark if you help people help themselves, gain confidence in their knowledge, and then engage more knowledgeably with the world. The right combination of voice, volume, and vulnerability can empower audiences, ignite their courage, and renew their trust. What will happen if you help your audience to be smarter consumers, smarter citizens, and more confident in their own wisdom? You may be surprised by their loyalty and enthusiasm, such as in the case of the more than half of British citizens who identify the NHS as their greatest point of civic pride—more so than British history, the Royal Family, or other areas of the culture.[8] You'll also help your customers make a bigger impact on the world themselves, like the small businesses that brought in nearly 840 million orders on the Mailchimp platform in 2019,[9] representing more than 60% of the email marketing industry.[10] What will happen if you empower and strengthen your audience, like the people who use Zoom to communicate with family, students, and colleagues, or the patients who use the Cancer Worksheets? You'll teach them how to be more secure and trust themselves— and you'll regain their trust as well. You'll affirm their hope. And you need to—for yourself, your organization, your users, and our society.

Let's get started.

Further reading

Alda, Alan. *If I Understood You, Would I Have This Look on My Face? My Adventures in the Art and Science of Relating and Communicating*. New York: Random House, 2017.

Bloomstein, Margot. *Content Strategy at Work: Real-World Stories to Strengthen Every Interactive Project*. Burlington, MA: Morgan Kaufmann Publishers, 2012.

Botsman, Rachel. *Who Can You Trust? How Technology Brought Us Together and Why It Might Drive Us Apart*. New York: PublicAffairs, 2017.

Carr, Nicholas. *The Shallows: What the Internet Is Doing to Our Brains*. New York: W.W. Norton & Company, 2011.

Doerr, John E. *Measure What Matters: How Google, Bono, and the Gates Foundation Rock the World with OKRs*. New York: Portfolio/Penguin, 2018.

Kovach, Bill, and Tom Rosenstiel. *Blur: How to Know What's True in the Age of Information Overload*. New York: Bloomsbury, 2015.

McCloud, Scott. *Understanding Comics: The Invisible Art*. New York: HarperCollins Publishers, 1994.

Nichols, Tom. *The Death of Expertise: The Campaign Against Established Knowledge and Why It Matters*. New York: Oxford University Press, 2017.

Oreskes, Naomi. *Why Trust Science?* Princeton, NJ: Princeton University Press, 2019.

Pillot de Chenecey, Sean. *The Post-Truth Business: How to Rebuild Brand Authenticity in a Distrusting World*. London: Kogan Page Inspire, 2019.

Pink, Daniel H. *When: The Scientific Secrets of Perfect Timing*. New York: Riverhead Books, 2017.

Thomas, David Dylan. *Design for Cognitive Bias*. New York: A Book Apart, 2020.

Wodtke, Christina. *Pencil Me In: The Business Drawing Book for People Who Can't Draw*. Palo Alto: Cucina Media, 2017.

Interviews cited

THANK YOU to the many people who kindly sat down with me for an interview. Your perspective illuminates my thinking, and I appreciate your candor and generosity.

Alexandra Chandler, previously the Democratic congressional candidate for Massachusetts Third Congressional District, currently a policy advocate with Protect Democracy; interview with the author, August 2018.

Amy Lenert, chief content officer at Crutchfield; interview with the author, December 2017.

Antonio de Luca, digital art director at *The New York Times*; interview with the author, November 2018.

April Starr, senior manager of experience research at Motorola Solutions and independent designer; interview with the author, February 2020.

Bill Smartt, president, Smartt Talk Inc.; interview with the author, December 2017.

Bonnie Dahan, previously senior vice president of creative at Banana Republic, currently strategic business development advisor at Bonnie Trust Dahan Consulting; interview with the author, August 2018.

Calla Rongerude, director of public education and communications at LGBT Movement Advancement Project and campaign director at Open to All; interview with the author, March 2020.

Christina Wodtke, independent consultant and lecturer at Stanford University; interview with the author, February 2020.

Christopher C. Maggiano, president, Cormier & Company; direct message exchange with the author, March 2020.

Dana Chisnell, previously co-executive director at the Center for Civic Design, currently founder and director of project redesign at the National Conference on Citizenship; direct message exchange with the author, April 2020.

Dean Vipond, digital lead designer at NHS; interview with the author, February 2020.

Diana Landau, previously catalogue editor at Banana Republic, currently communications consultant at Parlandau Communications; interview with the author, July 2018.

Emily McManus, previously managing editor of TED.com; currently managing editor of WaitWhat; interview with the author, January 2018.

Jack Bishop, chief creative officer at America's Test Kitchen; interview with the author, December 2017.

Jennifer Morrell, previously deputy of elections and recording of Arapahoe County, Colorado, currently consultant at Democracy Fund; interview with the author, March 2018.

Julie Govan, brand manager at Crutchfield; interview with the author, December 2017.

Kate Kiefer Lee, previously senior director of communications and currently vice president of corporate communications at Mailchimp; interview with the author, November 2017.

Lisa Tozzi, previously global news director at *BuzzFeed*, currently managing editor for news and operations with *The Markup*; email exchange with the author, March 2017.

Lynn Boyden, previously information architect at the University of Southern California, currently senior human-centered researcher at NASA Jet Propulsion Laboratory; interview with the author, October 2019.

Mark DiCristina, previously senior director of brand marketing at Mailchimp and currently vice president of brand and Mailchimp Studios; interview with the author, February 2018.

Matthew Curry, previously head of ecommerce at Lovehoney, currently lifestyle brand consultant; interview with the author, December 2017.

Nancy Friedman, previously editorial director at Banana Republic, currently chief wordworker at Wordworking; interview with the author, July 2018.

Nicole Fenton, previously content design supervisor at 18F, US General Services Administration, currently communications manager for Chorus at Vox Media and co-author of *Nicely Said*; interviews with the author, December 2017 and February to April 2020.

Sara Wilcox, digital content designer at NHS; interview with the author, February 2020.

Sarah Richards, previously head of content design at the Government Digital Service, currently founder of and principal consultant at Content Design London; interviews with the author, January to February 2018 and January 2020.

Shawn Sprockett, previously design lead at Airbnb, currently design director of emergent experiences at Godfrey Dadich Partners; interview with the author, February 2018.

Steve Kindig, senior home audio video editor at Crutchfield; interview with the author, November 2017.

Whitney Quesenbery, co-founder of the Center for Civic Design; interviews with the author, February 2018 and April 2020.

Notes

Chapter 1: Introduction

1 The team at GOV.UK cut the content to help users find conclusive answers, make decisions more easily, and gain confidence in information. Their investment in content design also makes maintenance and updating much easier for content contributors. Background came largely from a personal interview with Sarah Richards, the head of content design in Government Digital Services. The team condensed information from multiple government websites by limiting versions, determining what was most relevant to user needs, and designing it in the appropriate format. In an interview with Giles Turnbull for the GDS blog (*see* https://gds.blog.gov.uk/2014/03/14/what-we-mean-when-we-talk-about-content-design), Richards further describes the process:

> Traditionally you may have had an editorial team, but we want to distinguish the difference between just writing information and presenting the user with the best information possible. It's not just writing any more. We take a user need—so something that a user will need to find out from government—and we present it in the best way possible. That could be a calculator, a tool; it could be a video, it could be anything. It doesn't have to just be words. That's why we call it content design.

This example is representative of my process in this book: where possible, I conducted original research with the people who did the work and weighed the risks. Our discussions illuminated research with third-party resources, articles, and blog posts to offer lessons that transcend industries and budgets. And while brands' bad behavior often earns headlines, it's *good* work that we should emulate. I turned my attention to organizations that invest in fostering trust and building confidence in the hope that you will too.

Part I: Voice

1   Nicole Fenton and Kate Kiefer Lee, *Nicely Said: Writing for the Web with Style and Purpose* (San Francisco: New Riders, 2014), 61.

2   In *30 Rock*, season 1, episode 6, Liz Lemon asks her idiot boyfriend why he still holds on to a pager in an era of cell phones. "Technology is cyclical, Liz!" he retorts. Of course, in that case it's not true, but it's a comforting fantasy when the new model isn't nearly as good as what you already have.

3   In 1965, Fairchild Semiconductor's director of R&D, Gordon Moore, observed that the number of components on a dense integrated circuit doubled every year—and would likely continue at that pace. In 1975, several years after co-founding Intel, he revised his prediction to say that the number of transistors would double every two years. Moore's Law has become a dominant axiom of circuit design, propelling advancements in computing power in many industries.

Chapter 2: Communicate with consistency across time and channels

1   Mailchimp, "Mailchimp's Year in Review 2019, Market Share," https://mailchimp.com/annual-report/stats/market-share. As annual reports go, this one is dazzling. It's both full of surprises and no surprise at all: it embodies the brand's voice to be

informative, supportive, and fun. It reports on Mailchimp's performance by spotlighting the accomplishments of the company's
clients with style.

2 Mailchimp, "Mailchimp's Year in Review 2019, Active Customers,"
https://mailchimp.com/annual-report/stats/active-customers.

3 Designer Raymond Loewy articulated his MAYA—"most advanced,
yet acceptable"—principle through his work and in his autobi-
ography, *Never Leave Well Enough Alone* (1951; Baltimore, MD:
Johns Hopkins University Press, 2002). As designers, we often
strive to offer users a new vision for quotidian experiences and the
objects that are so familiar as to be invisible. But if your user looks
at a chair and doesn't know how or where to sit, she's not bringing
it home.

4 Erin Crews, "Voice and Tone Principles," Mailchimp internal docu-
mentation, October 2019.

5 Mailchimp, "Mailchimp Content Style Guide," https://styleguide.
mailchimp.com.

6 In *Content Strategy at Work: Real-World Stories to Strengthen
Every Interactive Project* (Burlington, MA: Morgan Kaufmann,
2012), I detail the process and impact of a message architecture.
It's a hierarchy of communication goals, or an outline, that reflects
an internal exercise around a constrained vocabulary. Using
BrandSort to facilitate the work, I guide my client team through
a three-step exercise. First, they sort the cards to reflect who they
are, who they're not, and who they'd like to be—those qualities that
the brand can own in the hearts and minds of their target audience
if our initiative is successful. Then we examine "who we are" and
"who we'd like to be," the current state and future state. I ask them
to consider what they want to hold on to moving forward, and
what qualities they can leave behind. This activity is aspirational,
and I want them to have big aspirations. Perhaps the company
has always been seen as traditional and stodgy, and now it's time
to spotlight their research and herald a new era of innovation!
Maybe they've always been known as a regional school, but new
recruiting and messaging means they want to emerge as a national

brand! Whatever the goal, they focus on developing that "we'd like to be" list. Finally, we take a hard look at the list and identify the emerging groups or patterns. Is there a group of terms that speaks to how they want to be known—say, as friendly, welcoming, and approachable? Is there another group that describes their entre-preneurial, innovative, savvy side? By clarifying and prioritizing those groups, we write a new story for the brand about what's most important to communicate, what comes next, and so on—and that's the message architecture. It's an actionable, internal tool that guides the work of designers, writers, and the entire UX and creative team.

7 In her expansive archive *Abandoned Republic*, Robyn Adams interviews illustrator Kevin Sarkki to bring behind-the-khaki commentary to the rich history of the beloved brand. If you have fond memories of the witty writing, intoxicating store décor, and impeccable pencil work, spend some time sifting through the treasures in her collection. *See* Robyn Adams, "Banana Republic Memories from Staff Artist Kevin Sarkki," *Abandoned Republic*, June 2, 2011, https://www.secretfanbase.com/banana/banana-republic-memories-from-staff-artist-kevin-sarkki.

8 The Climate Desk is discussed in Robyn Adams's "Memos to Kevin re: Banana Republic," *Abandoned Republic*, March 20, 2014, https://secretfanbase.com/banana/sarkki-memos/nggallery/image/the-climate-desk-1.

9 Elizabeth MacGowan, "The Banana Connection," *Backpacker Magazine*, September 1986, 13.

10 The J. Peterman Company, "Owner's Hat," J Peterman.com 2010–2011, accessed from the Internet Archive, http://web.archive.org/web/20100723052225/http:/www.jpeterman.com/mens-accessories/owners-hat.

Chapter 3: Educate with humility and transparency

1 James Comey, "Message from the Director," 2015 Crime in the United States, Criminal Justice Information Services Division,

https://ucr.fbi.gov/crime-in-the-u.s/2015/crime-in-the-u.s.-2015/
resource-pages/messagefromthedirector_final.

2 In her role at 18F, Nicole Fenton coached a distributed team of
writers and content designers across a range of assignments. She
personally led interviews, testing, and content design work for the
FBI Crime Data Explorer. Following her tour of duty with GSA,
Nicole joined Vox Media, where she is the principal community
manager for the Chorus publishing platform.

Chapter 4: Use plain language to build confidence

1 Henry David Thoreau, *Walden* (1854; New York: Book of the
Month Club, 1996), 119.

2 Albert Einstein actually said, "It can scarcely be denied that the
supreme goal of all theory is to make the irreducible basic elements
as simple and as few as possible without having to surrender the
adequate representation of a single datum of experience," but it
was composer Roger Sessions who made Einstein's remarks as
simple, and quotable, as possible. Writing in *The New York Times*
on January 8, 1950, Sessions commented, "I also remember a
remark of Albert Einstein, which certainly applies to music. He
said, in effect, that everything should be as simple as it can be
but not simpler!" The craft of visual communication, like music,
demands attention to detail: communicate specifically and clearly
to articulate the most complex concepts in their most refined state
of simplicity.

3 ClinicalTrials.gov, "Study to Assess the Safety and Effects of
Cells Injected Intravitreal in Dry Macular Degeneration," US
National Library of Medicine, https://clinicaltrials.gov/ct2/show/
NCT02024269.

4 Ajay E. Kuriyan, Thomas A. Albini, Justin H. Townsend, Marianeli
Rodriguez, Hemang K. Pandya, Robert E. Leonard, II, M. Brandon
Parrott, Philip J. Rosenfeld, Harry W. Flynn, Jr., and Jeffrey L.
Goldberg, "Vision Loss After Intravitreal Injection of Autologous
'Stem Cells' for AMD," *New England Journal of Medicine* 376,
March 2017, DOI: 10.1056/NEJMoa1609583.

5   National Health Service, "NHS Service Standard: Make Sure
    Everyone Can Use the Service," Digital Service Manual, https://
    service-manual.nhs.uk/service-standard/5-make-sure-
    everyone-can-use-the-service.

6   Hugh Rayner, Michael Rosen, and Sara Wilcox, *Word of Mouth*,
    BBC Radio 4, January 28, 2020, https://www.bbc.co.uk/
    programmes/mooodpkc.

7   National Health Service, "NHS Service Standard: Make the Service
    Simple to Use," Digital Service Manual, https://service-manual.nhs.
    uk/service-standard/5-make-sure-everyone-can-use-the-service.

8   Hannah Smith Allen, "Yunghi Kim on Intimacy in Photojourna-
    lism," *Popular Photography*, January 12, 2016, https://www.
    popphoto.com/american-photo/yunghi-kim-on-intimacy-in-
    photojournalism.

9   GOV.UK, "The NHS Constitution for England," Department of
    Health & Social Care, updated October 14, 2015, https://www.gov.
    uk/government/publications/the-nhs-constitution-for-england/
    the-nhs-constitution-for-england.

10 National Health Service, "How We Write," NHS Digital Service
    Manual, Content Style Guide, https://service-manual.nhs.uk/
    content/how-we-write.

11 Along with being senior manager of experience research at
    Motorola Solutions, April Starr is also the designer of the Cancer
    Worksheets (https://www.cancerworksheets.com/). Designers see
    the world as it is and believe it can be better, deploying a range
    of experience, skills, connections, and craft on issues and objects
    other people shrug off as "good enough" or "how it's always been."
    April embodies this practice throughout her work, and particularly
    in this project, which has attracted the attention of doctors and
    patients alike. Because she believed the patient experience could
    be better, today it is. To find out more about April and her project,
    see Mark Wilson, "This Designer Lost Her Husband to Cancer.
    Now She's Helping Others Cope—Through Design," *Fast Company*,
    February 25, 2020, https://www.fastcompany.com/90467322/

this-designer-lost-her-husband-to-cancer-now-shes-helping-others-cope-through-design.

Part II: Volume

1 Lisa Eadicicco, "Apple Stores Make an Insane Amount of Money," *Time*, May 18, 2016, https://time.com/4339170/apple-store-sales-comparison.

2 Patagonia, "How We're Reducing Our Carbon Footprint," https://www.patagonia.com/stories/how-were-reducing-our-carbon-footprint/story-74099.html.

Chapter 5: Share your work and remove all doubt

1 America's Test Kitchen, *What Good Cooks Know: 20 Years of Test Kitchen Expertise in One Essential Handbook* (Brookline, MA: America's Test Kitchen, 2016), 172. Even if you don't cook, it's fascinating to explore the Test Kitchen's process.

2 America's Test Kitchen, "The Best of Our Favorite (and Least Favorite) Food Processors," *Cook's Illustrated*, January 2016, https://www.cooksillustrated.com/equipment_reviews/2194-food-processors.

3 Andrew Janjigian, "Best Ground Beef Chili Recipe," *Cook's Illustrated*, November 2015, https://www.cooksillustrated.com/articles/32-best-ground-beef-chili-recipe.

4 America's Test Kitchen, "Millionaire's Shortbread," *Cook's Illustrated*, November/December 2016, https://www.cooksillustrated.com/recipes/9253-millionaires-shortbread. Like shortbread? Me neither. But if you're swayed by chewy-gooey caramel and chocolate, you'll *love* this shortbread.

5 For an example of how American's Test Kitchen uses social media to build on the show and magazine, see a behind-the-scenes shot of a team member preparing Millionaire's Shortbread on Twitter at https://twitter.com/TestKitchen/status/710452237097684993.

6 Steve Kindig, "Transforming a Basement into a Home Theater," Crutchfield, https://www.crutchfield.com/learn/transforming-basement-to-home-theater.html.

7 Deia Zukowski, "How to Choose the Best DSLR Camera for a Beginner," Crutchfield, https://www.crutchfield.com/learn/how-to-choose-the-best-DSLR-camera-for-a-beginner.html.

Chapter 6: Say what you have to say, then stop

1 In 2010, Sarah Richards saw that content resources needed to address bigger issues. Rather than focus primarily on grammar, style, and maintenance, she thought they should be addressing formative challenges in what the government should publish, why, and how. Her advocacy informed the structure and scope of the Government Digital Service content design team. Sarah now consults with governments, charities, and organizations worldwide on issues in content strategy and content design as the founding principal of Content Design London.

2 GOV.UK, "Working When Pregnant," Direct.gov, January 7, 2008, accessed via the National Archives, https://webarchive.national archives.gov.uk/20111030142815/http://www.direct.gov.uk/prod_consum_dg/idcplg?IdcService=SS_GET_PAGE&SsDocName=DG_10026556&IS_SSPU=1.

3 GOV.UK, "Guidance: Government Design Principles," Government Digital Service, last updated September 10, 2019, https://www.gov.uk/guidance/government-design-principles.

4 BeeBase, National Bee Unit, Animal & Plant Health Agency, http://www.nationalbeeunit.com.

5 GOV.UK, "Bumblebees: Licence to Release Non-Native Species in Commercial Premises for Research (CL34)," https://www.gov.uk/government/publications/bumblebees-licence-to-release-non-native-species-in-commercial-premises-for-research.

6 GOV.UK, "UK Trade Tariff, Chapter 9 – Coffee, Tea, Maté and Spices," Government Digital Service Blog, August 6, 2012,

https://gds.blog.gov.uk/wp-content/uploads/sites/60/2012/08/
uktt-old-coffee.png.

7   GOV.UK, "Trade Tariff, Beta, Coffee, Tea, Maté, and Spices,
Government Digital Service Blog, August 6, 2012, https://gds.blog.
gov.uk/wp-content/uploads/sites/60/2012/08/uktt-coffee.png.

8   GOV.UK, "Trade Tariff: Look Up Commodity Codes, Duty and VAT
Rates," https://www.gov.uk/trade-tariff.

9   GOV.UK, "Commodity Information for 5005001010," http://trade-
tariff.service.gov.uk/commodities/5005001010.

10   GOV.UK, "Claim Child Benefit," https://www.gov.uk/child-benefit.

11   GOV.UK, "Content Design: Planning, Writing, and Managing
Content," https://www.gov.uk/guidance/content-design/
what-is-content-design.

12   Ben Terrett, "A Few Notes on Typography," Government Digital
Service Blog, GOV.UK, July 5, 2012, https://gds.blog.gov.
uk/2012/07/05/a-few-notes-on-typography.

13   GOV.UK, "Guidance: Government Design Principles."

Chapter 7: Balance fidelity and abstraction to inform beyond the facts

1   Scraps from the Loft, "*John Mulaney: Kid Gorgeous at Radio City*
(2018)–Full Transcript," May 5, 2018, http://scrapsfromtheloft
.com/2018/05/05/john-mulaney-kid-gorgeous-at-radio-city-
full-transcript.

2   Sententiae Antiquae, "What Is Believed Overpowers the Truth:
Sophoklean Fragments on Lies and Truth," June 23, 2015,
https://sententiaeantiquae.com/2015/06/23/what-is-believed-
overpowers-the-truth-sophoklean-fragments-on-lies-and-truth.

3   Richard Saul Wurman, *Tokyo Access* (Los Angeles: Access Press, 1984).

4   Paul Watzlawick, Janet Beavin Bavelas, and Don D. Jackson,
*Pragmatics of Human Communication: A Study of Interna-
tional Patterns, Pathologies, and Paradoxes* (New York: W.W.
Norton, 1967).

5 Richard Saul Wurman, *Information Anxiety* (New York: Doubleday, 1989).

6 Center for Civic Design, "About," https://civicdesign.org/about.

7 Alexandra Chandler was the first transgender person to run for national office from Massachusetts and one of the first transgender people in the US intelligence community to transition on the job.

Chapter 8: Convene community
for collaborative creation

1 Don Norman, "Design Thinking: A Useful Myth," *Core77*, June 25, 2010, https://www.core77.com/posts/16790/design-thinking-a-useful-myth-16790.

2 Penzeys Spices, "A comment of hope..." Facebook, October 30, 2018, https://www.facebook.com/Penzeys/posts/10156948198177834?comment_id=10156948409122834.

3 Penzeys Spices, "Dear CEO..." Facebook, December 1, 2016, https://www.facebook.com/Penzeys/photos/a.10154182484242834/10154815494657834.

4 Global Strategy Group, "Doing Business in an Activist World: Sixth Annual Business & Politics Study," February 2019, http://globalstrategygroup.com/wp-content/uploads/2019/02/GSG-2019_doing-business-in-an-activist-world_business-and-politics.pdf.

5 Elizabeth B.-N. Sanders, "Converging Perspectives: Product Development Research for the 1990s," *Design Management Journal* 3(4), Fall 1992, DOI: 10.1111/j.1948-7169.1992.tb00604.x.

6 Edelman, "Edelman Earned Brand 2018," October 2, 2018, https://www.edelman.com/earned-brand.

7 Richard Ralphsmith, "Australian Brands Have Gone Political, but It's Time to Step Outside the 'Zone of Acceptability,'" *Mumbrella*, March 20, 2018, https://mumbrella.com.au/australian-brands-have-gone-political-but-its-time-to-step-outside-the-zone-of-acceptability-505985.

Chapter 9: Lean into the lessons of what went wrong

1 The White House, "Coronavirus Guidelines for America," March 16, 2020, https://www.whitehouse.gov/briefings-statements/coronavirus-guidelines-america.

2 Santa Clara County Public Health, "County of Santa Clara Public Health Department Reports Third Case of COVID-19," February 28, 2020, https://www.sccgov.org/sites/phd/news/Pages/third-novel-coronavirus-case-02-2020.aspx.

3 The White House, "Proclamation on Suspension of Entry as Immigrants and Nonimmigrants of Persons Who Pose a Risk of Transmitting 2019 Novel Coronavirus," January 31, 2020, https://www.whitehouse.gov/presidential-actions/proclamation-suspension-entry-immigrants-nonimmigrants-persons-pose-risk-transmitting-2019-novel-coronavirus.

4 Fiona Kelliher, "Coronavirus: First Case Confirmed in Santa Clara County," *The Mercury News*, January 31, 2020, https://www.mercurynews.com/2020/01/31/santa-clara-coronavirus.

5 County of Santa Clara Public Health Department, "Health Officer Order to Shelter in Place," https://www.sccgov.org/sites/covid19/documents/03-16-20-health-officer-order-to-shelter-in-place.pdf.

6 Federal Motor Carrier Safety Administration, "California Governor Newsom Executive Order-N33-20," https://www.fmcsa.dot.gov/emergency/california-governor-newsom-shelter-place-executive-order-n33-20.

7 Julia Prodis Sulek, "Meet the Doctor Who Ordered the Bay Area's Coronavirus Lockdown, the First in the U.S.," *The Mercury News*, March 29, 2020, https://www.mercurynews.com/2020/03/29/she-shut-down-the-bay-area-to-slow-the-deadly-coronavirus-none-of-us-really-believed-we-would-do-it.

8 Elizabeth Cushing, "Our Approach to Disclosure of Medical Error and Compensation," CRICO, May 29, 2012, https://rmf.harvard.edu/clinician-resources/article/2012/CRICOs-approach-to-disclosure-of-medical-error-and-compensation.

9 Tom A. Augello, "Surgeons and Error Disclosure," *Patient Safety Updates*, 10:01, CRICO Podcast, July 1, 2006, https://rmf.harvard.edu/clinician-resources/podcast/2006/surgeons-and-error-disclosure.

10 D.K. Chan, T.H. Gallagher, R. Reznick, and W. Levinson, "How Surgeons Disclose Medical Errors to Patients: A Study Using Standardized Patients," *Surgery* 138(5), November 2005, DOI: 10.1016/j.surg.2005.04.015.

11 Augello, "Surgeons and Error Disclosure."

12 Matthew McLachlan and Mark McLachlan, "Fidget Cube: A Vinyl Desk Toy," Kickstarter, https://www.kickstarter.com/projects/antsylabs/fidget-cube-a-vinyl-desk-toy.

13 Matthew McLachlan and Mark McLachlan, "Production, Shipping Timeline, and Other News!" Kickstarter, December 7, 2016, https://www.kickstarter.com/projects/antsylabs/fidget-cube-a-vinyl-desk-toy/posts/1758915.

14 Matthew McLachlan and Mark McLachlan, "Happy New Year + Shipping Update," Kickstarter, January 4, 2017, https://www.kickstarter.com/projects/antsylabs/fidget-cube-a-vinyl-desk-toy/posts/1777532.

15 Matthew McLachlan and Mark McLachlan, "January Shipping Update, Fidget Family Spotlight, and More!" Kickstarter, January 26, 2017, https://www.kickstarter.com/projects/antsylabs/fidget-cube-a-vinyl-desk-toy/posts/1792750.

16 Matthew McLachlan and Mark McLachlan, "Communication, Shipping Updates, and Fidget Family Spotlight!" Kickstarter, March 2, 2017, https://www.kickstarter.com/projects/antsylabs/fidget-cube-a-vinyl-desk-toy/posts/1821396.

17 Matthew McLachlan and Mark McLachlan, "Introducing... Fidget Cube Collectibles," Kickstarter, January 2, 2018, https://www.kickstarter.com/projects/antsylabs/fidget-cube-a-vinyl-desk-toy/posts/2082389.

18 Michael V. Copeland, "Pseudoscience Saps the Power of TEDx Brand," *Wired*, December 7, 2012, https://www.wired.com/2012/12/pseudo-science-saps-the-power-of-tedx.

19 Evgeny Morozov, "The Naked and the TED," *The New Republic*, August 2, 2012, https://newrepublic.com/article/105703/the-naked-and-the-ted-khanna.

20 Nilofer Merchant, "When TED Lost Control of Its Crowd," *Harvard Business Review*, April 2013, https://hbr.org/2013/04/when-ted-lost-control-of-its-crowd.

21 TED, "Dimitar Sasselov, TED Global 2010: How We Found Hundreds of Potential Earth-Like Planets," July 2010, https://www.ted.com/talks/dimitar_sasselov_how_we_found_hundreds_of_potential_earth_like_planets.

22 Gap Inc., "Inclusion, by Design," https://www.gapinc.com/en-us/values/diversity-inclusion.

23 Gap Inc., "Measuring Our Progress," https://www.gapincsustainability.com/measuring-our-progress.

24 Old Navy, "Earlier this week…" Facebook, February 3, 2018, https://www.facebook.com/oldnavy/posts/10155088260692021.

25 Eric S. Yuan, "A Message to Our Users," Zoom, April 1, 2020, https://blog.zoom.us/a-message-to-our-users.

26 Taylor Lorenz, "'Zoombombing': When Video Conferences Go Wrong," *The New York Times*, March 20, 2020, https://www.nytimes.com/2020/03/20/style/zoombombing-zoom-trolling.html.

Chapter 10: Vision for the future

1 Henry Rollins, *Provoked*, 2.13.61, Inc., 2008, audio CD. While Theodore Roosevelt, Erica Jong, and many others expressed this same belief, what we need most now is the vigorous energy and DIY sensibility of punk musician Rollins. Sowing hope and empowering others takes energy, and we are all responsible for doing the work.

2 Pew Research Center, "Americans' Confidence That Scientists Act in the Public Interest Is up Since 2016," February 11, 2020, https://www.pewresearch.org/fact-tank/2020/02/12/key-findings-about-americans-confidence-in-science-and-their-views-on-scientists-role-in-society/ft_2020-02-12_aaasroundup_04.

3   Matthew Goldberg, Abel Gustafson, Seth Rosenthal, John
    Kotcher, Edward Malbach, and Anthony Leiserowitz, "For the
    First Time, the Alarmed Are Now the Largest of Global Warming's
    Six Americas," Yale Program on Climate Change Communication,
    January 16, 2020, https://climatecommunication.yale.edu/
    publications/for-the-first-time-the-alarmed-are-now-the-largest-
    of-global-warmings-six-americas.

4   Sleeping Giants is a social media activism organization that aims to
    persuade brands to stop advertising with and funding news outlets
    that give a platform to racist, sexist, xenophobic, homophobic, or
    anti-Semitic reporting and editorial content. It launched in 2016
    to draw attention to advertisers on Breitbart News Network. Their
    campaigns may have caught the attention of both a newly mobi-
    lized audience and advertisers alike, as many expressed surprise
    that their ads underwrote content through programmatic adver-
    tising, ad placements that targets audience segments instead of
    specific sites. Armed with that information, Sleeping Giants mobi-
    lized a grassroots campaign to alert advertisers to their presence
    on Breitbart that resulted in hundreds of companies pulling their
    ads from the site (*see* https://www.facebook.com/slpnggiants).

    The grassroots #GrabYourWallet boycott on Twitter was
    launched in 2016 by Shannon Coulter and Sue Atencio in response
    to Donald Trump's presidential campaign. Echoing the candidate's
    lewd denigration of women, the boycott targeted Trump brand
    retailers that profited from the campaign's racism, xenophobia,
    and sexism. For the first three years, the Grab Your Wallet website
    offered a real-time listing of which companies still carried Trump
    brand products. It encouraged visitors to contact companies,
    respectfully express their concerns, and refrain from doing busi-
    ness with them until they severed financial ties with the Trump
    brand. The boycott was visible and successful, driving 70 compa-
    nies to drop the Trump brand. Now a 501c4 nonprofit, Grab Your
    Wallet evolved into a more general resource to help people flex
    their economic power in ways that promote equity and respect
    (*see* https://www.grabyourwallet.org).

5 Molly McLaughlin and Brian T. Horowitz, "Mailchimp Review,"
   PCMag, October 31, 2019, https://www.pcmag.com/reviews/
   mailchimp.
6 Mailchimp, "Mailchimp Transparency Report," https://mailchimp.
   com/transparency-report.
7 Jacob Elson, "Customer Data Killed the Shopify-Mailchimp
   Partnership," *Ecommerce Magazine*, March 27, 2019, https://
   www.ecommerce-mag.com/customer-data-killed-the-shopify-
   mailchimp-partnership.
8 Mintel Press Office, "UK British Lifestyles Market Report," June 7,
   2018, https://www.mintel.com/press-centre/social-and-lifestyle/
   british-lifestyles-the-nhs-tops-list-of-uks-most-cherished-
   institutions.
9 Mailchimp, "Annual Report, 2019, Ecommerce Orders," https://
   mailchimp.com/annual-report/stats/unique-email-addresses.
10 Datanyze, "Market Share, Emailing Marketing," https://www.
   datanyze.com/market-share/email-marketing--13.

Figures

2.1 Screen captures from Mailchimp, "The Beginning of Freddie &
    Co.," https://mailchimp.com/resources/issue-1-idea; Mailchimp,
    "Meg's Freddie & Co. Recap," https://mailchimp.com/resources/
    issue-37-freddie-co-recap.
2.2 Photograph by Mel Ziegler, "Before Banana Republic Was Main-
    stream Fashion, It Was a Weirdly Wonderful Safari Brand," *Adweek*,
    March 16, 2016, https://www.adweek.com/brand-marketing/
    banana-republic-was-mainstream-fashion-it-was-weirdly-
    wonderful-safari-brand-170059.
2.3 Men's Authentic Ticking Shirt, Banana Republic Travel & Safari
    Clothing Co. catalogue, fall 1987, 62.
3.1 Koss ad, Koss, https://www.koss.com/history.
3.2 Vibebot chat window, Lovehoney, https://www.lovehoney.com/
    vibebot.

3.3   Screen capture from the Crime Data Explorer, Clark County School District, Federal Bureau of Investigation, https://crime-data-explorer.fr.cloud.gov/explorer/agency/NV0021600/crime.

4.1   NHS advisory pop-ups, National Health Service, https://service-manual.nhs.uk/design-system/components/warning-callout; https://service-manual.nhs.uk/design-system/components/care-cards.

5.1   Pages from *Cook's Illustrated*, November/December 2010, 16–17.

5.2   America's Test Kitchen Twitter post, March 17, 2016, https://twitter.com/TestKitchen/status/710452237097684993.

6.1   Screen capture from the "Working When Pregnant" web pages, GOV.UK, January 7, 2008, accessed via the National Archives, https://webarchive.nationalarchives.gov.uk/20111030142815/http://www.direct.gov.uk/prod_consum_dg/idcplg?IdcService=SS_GET_PAGE&SsDocName=DG_10026556&IS_SSPU=1.

6.2   Screen capture from Business Link, Government Digital Service Blog, GOV.UK, August 6, 2012, https://gds.blog.gov.uk/wp-content/uploads/sites/60/2012/08/uktt-old-coffee.png.

6.3   Screen capture of trade tariff information, GOV.UK, https://www.gov.uk/trade-tariff.

6.4   Screen capture of tariffs for commodity 5005001010 (yarn spun from silk waste, not put up for retail sale) from GOV.UK, https://www.trade-tariff.service.gov.uk/commodities/5005001010.

6.5   Screen capture of information on claiming the Child Benefit, GOV.UK, https://www.gov.uk/child-benefit.

7.1   Illustration by Margot Bloomstein.

7.2   Instruction slip from an Arapahoe County ballot package, Center for Civic Design, https://civicdesign.org/wp-content/uploads/2017/03/showcase-stub3-600x67.png.

8.1   Photograph by Bayeté Ross Smith, "Hyphen-Nation," *The New York Times*, https://www.nytimes.com/interactive/projects/storywall/hyphen-nation.

8.2 Top: illustration by Andre Piron, *Frankfurter Allgemeine Zeitung*, https://www.faz.net/aktuell/wirtschaft/digitec/chinas-internet-im-ueberblick-16411163.html; bottom: Illustration by Josh Cochran, "Hyphen-Nation," *The New York Times*, https://www.nytimes.com/interactive/projects/storywall/hyphen-nation.

8.3 Screen shot from Penzeys' sales chart, Penzeys, Facebook, https://www.facebook.com/Penzeys/photos/a.10154182484242834/10156645940752834.

9.1 Screen shot from the web page for Dimitar Sasselov's July 2010 TED talk, TED, https://www.ted.com/talks/dimitar_sasselov_how_we_found_hundreds_of_potential_earth_like_planets.

Acknowledgments
and appreciation

LET ME be clear, detailed, and vulnerable: so many people have offered feedback, introduced colleagues, and given me a platform to ask questions and share my ideas. If I'm able to see far, it's because I stand on the shoulders of giants.

Thank you to the conference and event organizers and attendees who let me develop these ideas on the stage. Kristina Halvorson, Tenessa Gemelke, and the Confab family, your guidance is gold; thank you for building such a collaborative community. Jeffrey Zeldman, Eric Meyer, and everyone at An Event Apart, thank you for letting me bring my experience to a broader audience. SXSW, Design & Content Conference, Content Marketing Conference, Women Talk Design, OmnichannelX, Fluxible, UX in the City, World Interaction Design Day, World Information Architecture Day Boston, and UIE: thank you for trusting me with your audience.

To go far, go together. I appreciate traveling through this world with the folks of Camp Contentment. Jennifer Jeffrey,

Rick Allen, Corey Vilhauer, Keri Maijala, Eileen Webb, Steve
Fisher, Lisa Maria Marquis, Sara Wachter-Boettcher, thank
you for offering just the feedback I needed when I needed it
most! Ladyslack, thank you for giving me your savvy, cheer-
leading, and silence, all in equal measure. Coffee and Cotton
and Mill City Cheesemongers at Mill No. 5, thank you for giving me the space to focus amid the buzz of community. Amy
Thibodeau and Dan Zambonini, merci pour Bize, l'endroit où
j'ai écrit ces idées pour la première fois.

Generous introductions, feedback, and perspective from
people with experience beyond my own expanded the breadth
of this book. You'll hear many of their voices in these pages.
Chris Avore, Tonia Bartz, Lynn Boyden, Anita Cheng, Dana
Chisnell, Bedirhan Cinar, Jonathon Colman, Erin Crews, Karen
Dawson, Kara DeFrias, Katie Del Angel, Christian DeLisle,
Kataryna Lyson DeLisle, Sophie Dennis, Jeff Eaton, Nicole
Fenton, Katherine Gray, Matthew Grocki, Erika Hall, Carrie
Hane, Kevin Hoffman, Jevaun Howell, Aaron Irizarry, Denise
Jacobs, Kate Kiefer Lee, Ahava Leibtag, Donna Lichaw, Oliver
Lindberg, Jeffrey MacIntyre, Farai Madzima, Chris Maggiano,
Karen McGrane, Kate O'Neill, Laura Gassner Otting, Lynne
Polischuik, Sarah Richards, Liz Robinson, Brenda Sanderson,
Melanie Seibert, Tanya Snook, Samantha Soma, April Starr,
Wendy Stengel, Vicky Teinaki, Cathy Terwilliger, Amy Thibo-
deau, David Dylan Thomas, Gretchen Thomas, Noz Urbina,
Tamsen Webster, Andy Welfle, Heinz Wittenbrink, Christina
Wodtke, Carolyn Wood—thank you for answering my late-
night emails and even later DMs.

Jeff Shreve, thank you for your early enthusiasm and direction for the shape of this work.

Josh Silverman, my world would be so much smaller if we had never met. Thank you for the introductions, opportunities, good ideas, and even better puns.

Trena, Caela, Amanda, Peter, Annemarie, Melissa, Alison, and the entire team at Page Two, thank you for investing your time, creativity, and talent in this work. I am so honored to have your partnership in bringing these ideas to life.

Jill Swenson, you are relentless and unforgiving. Editing is an act of love; thank you for the tough love. You championed my ideas and voice through my fear, doubt, and dreck. Thank you on behalf of everyone who reads my words.

Mom and Dad, thank you for the endless encouragement, childcare, and support that allowed me to put my attention into this work. By your example, I believe in both the work of opportunity and the luck of possibility.

Clover, thank you for asking big questions and engaging me with big answers. The only thing more fun than designing our way to a better world is exploring it with you and Deedee.

Mike, thank you for listening to the first draft of my ideas and challenging me to think harder before I bring them to the page or stage. When the wind whistles through my drafts like they are mere scaffolding for bigger visions, you hold faith and space with those visions and make the time in our lives to let them thrive. Thank you for trusting me, loving me, and making us dinner.

Index

Note: Page numbers in *italics* refer
to figures; page numbers followed
by *n* refer to note numbers

Abandoned Republic, 33, 224*n*7
abstraction, 6, 131–33, 137–39,
150–51
actionable communication, 132
active voice, 60–61, 73
activism, 168, *169*, 170–71, 193,
234*n*4
Airbnb, 139–40
algorithms, 205
AMD (age-related macular degeneration), 64
America's Test Kitchen, 5, 90–96, *97*,
98–99, 102, 109, 121, 128. *See
also Cook's Illustrated*
Amsterdam Airport Schiphol, 72
analysis paralysis, 111
Antsy Labs, 181–87, 195, 200
ANZ Bank, 171
API (application programming
interface), 51
Apple, 14, 85–86

appliance sales, 45
Arapahoe County Clerk's Office,
143–45; ballots, *145*
arrogance, 41, 45
assumptions, 56
audiences, 8, 212; alienating, 17,
41–42, 164; awareness of, 94;
loyalty of, 18; respecting, 164;
trusting, 203–4
Australian Football League, 171
authenticity, 6–7, 34, 141, 200

Backpacker Magazine, 35
Banana Republic, 3, 28–38, *34*,
39, 85
Bay Area, 200
BBC, 112, 121, 124
bees, 113–14
behaviors, doubling down on, 173
beliefs, lack of, 1
Best Buy, 86, 103
beta-launches, 46
Bishop, Jack, 93, 95–96, 98–99
blog posts, 5, *24*, 25, 69, 72, 83–84,
114, 126, 197–98, 210, 221–22*n*1

boundaries, 43–44, 57
brands, 154, 165; and activism, 167–68, *169*; evolving, 14–15; and voice, 2–4, 12, 41; and vulnerability, 7–8, 154–55
BrandSort, 223–24n6
breadmaking, 94–95
brevity, 109–10
Brexit, 114, 120
British government. *See* UK government

California Voter Bill of Rights, 142–43
callouts, 27, 71
Calvert, Margaret, 126
cancer, 75–77
Cancer Worksheets, 77–78, 136–37, 178, 211, 226–27n11
carbon neutrality, 86
catalogues: Banana Republic, 29, 31, *39*; Crutchfield, 101–2
Center for Civic Design, 142–43, 145
Chandler, Alexandra, 6, 146–50
chatbots, 45–48, *49*, 66
Chicago, 159
Child Benefit (UK), 122, *123*
Child, Julia, *93*
Chūō-Sōbu Line, 133
Clark County, Nevada, *55*
CliffsNotes, 137
climate change, 205
Climate Desk, 35
ClinicalTrials.gov, 63–67, 78
Cochran, Josh, *162*
Cody, Dr. Sara, 8, 175–79
collaborative creation, 159–61

comedians, 109
Comey, James, 50
communication, 14, 183–85, 187, 200
community-building, 166–69, 209
Compartment T, 148–50
compassion, 166
concept models, 133–34, *135*
confidence, 78–79, 83; building, 2–4, 59–60, 100, 117, 127; and success, 95; and trust, 83, 136, 151
Conley, James, 194, 196
consistency, 19, 124, 147
consultative sales, 44–45
Consumer Financial Protection Bureau, 206
content: amount of, 5–6, 82, 109; in chunks, 66; Crutchfield's, 103–5; dating, *191*, 192; enough, 83–86, 110–11, 128–29; producer/consumer relationships, 158–59; visual, 85
content creation/curation, 69–70
content design, 53
content strategy, 2, 63, 200, 228n1; brand-driven, 6, 30, 114–15; need-driven, 114; slow, 107
context, and delivery format, 98
convenience stores, 107
conversations, 67
Cook's Illustrated, *90*, 93, 96, *97*, 98, 104. *See also* America's Test Kitchen
Coopers Brewery, 171
Copeland, Michael V., 189
copywriting, 31, 115
coronavirus, 8, 174–78, 197, 200

COVID-19. *See* coronavirus
CRICO (Controlled Risk Insurance
  Company), 179–80, 183
Crime Data Explorer, 51–54, *55*,
  56–57, 62
Cronkite, Walter, 204–5
crowdfunding. *See* Kickstarter
Crutchfield, 99–109, 128, 209, 211
curation, 69
Curry, Matthew, 44, 46–47
customer support, 26
customers: concerns of, 19;
  Crutchfield's, 100–1, 106; views
  on, 18
cynicism, 1, 205, 210–12

Dahan, Bonnie, 30–32, 34–35
Dana Farber, 76
Daniel, Lucas, 75–77
data-sharing, 54
de Luca, Antonio, 159–61
democracy, 142
Department of Defense (US), 146–51
design thinking, 163–64
details, 82; from America's Test
  Kitchen, 94
dialogue, 65, 163
DiCristina, Mark, 20–22, 26–27
digital chat features, 44
digital literacy, 68
dot-gov domains, 63–65
dropdown menus, 54

eBay, 137, 182
ecommerce, 5, 26, 44, 208
Edelman Earned Brand Study, 170
Einstein, Albert, 62, 225*n2*

emojis, 48
empathy, 138–39, 165–66
empowerment, 73
enough, 84, 86, 110–11, 128–29
Erd, Patty and Tom, 168
expertise, sharing, 89

Facebook, 21
familiarity, importance of, 14
FAQs, 143
FBI, 3–4, 50–54, 59
FDA (Federal Drug Administra-
  tion), 63
fear, 2
feedback, 209
Fenton, Nicole, 13, 51–52, 54–55,
  62–63, 65–67, 225*n2*
fidelity, 132, 138, 150–51
Fidget Cubes, 181–86
first-person research, 99–104
footnotes, 192
Frankfurter Allgemeine Zeitung, 162
Freddie and Co., *24, 25*
Friedman, Nancy, 37
Frutiger, Adrian, 72
Frutiger (typeface), 72

Gallagher, Thomas, 179
Gap Inc., 28, 193, 195
gender, 148
General Services Administration
  (US), 62
Georgia (typeface), 126
Gill Sans (typeface), 72, 126
Global Strategy Group, 169
Govan, Julie, 105–7
government content, 65, 111, *112*,
  113, 115

Government Design Principles,
    113–16, 128
Government Digital Service (GDS),
    111, 115–16, 120, 124–25, 228n1
GOV.UK, 6, 72, 110–11, *112*, 113–17,
    118–19, *121*, 122, *123*, 124–28,
    221–22n1
Grab Your Wallet, 206, 234n4
graphic language, 53
grey, 127
growth, 17, 41, 206
guided shopping wizards, 45–48, *49*

health literacy, 68–69
healthcare, patient involvement, 166
Helvetica (typeface), 126
honesty, 50
hope, 2, 205, 210–12
humanization, 104–6, 211
humility, 42–43, 158, 163
"Hyphen-Nation", *160*, 161, *162*, 166

IDEO, 164
IKEA, 53
illustration, and storytelling, 32
image galleries, 5
images, 96, 105; and content
    creation, 69–70
inclusivity, 36
inconsistent reporting, of crime,
    55–56, *55*
infographics, 5, 53, 62, 100, 114
information, too much, 84
Instagram, 96
intellectuals, distrust of, 205–6
inter-departmental trust, 177

J. Peterman, 36–38
jargon, 4, 21, 52–53, 72, 76, 94
JFK International Airport, 72
Johnston Sans (typeface), 126

Kickstarter, 8, 181–86
Kid Gorgeous, 131
Kiefer Lee, Kate, 13, 18–20, 23, 26
Kim, Yunghi, 70
Kindig, Steve, 100–5
Kinneir, Jock, 126
knowledge: gaining, 45, 87; lack of,
    75–76
Koss, 42, *43*

Landau, Diana, 29, 32
law enforcement agencies, 50–52
Lenert, Amy, 108
Levinson, Wendy, 180
Lewinsky, Monica, 189
Loewy, Raymond, 19, 223n3
London Underground, 126
Lonely Planet, 38
longform copy, 82, 100
Lovehoney, 3–4, 44–48, *49*, 50, 54,
    57, 59, 209
loyalty: audience, 18; earning, 89

magalogues, 101
Magnolia Home Theaters, 103
Mailchimp, 3, 18–22, *24*, 25–28, 38,
    206–9, 213
maps, 6, 133–35
mascots, 20, 26
MAYA principle, 19, 223n3
McLachlan, Mark, 181, 186
McLachlan, Matthew, 181, 186

McLaughlin, Molly, 207
McManus, Emily, 188–90, 192
medical advisors, 67
medical errors, 179–80
medical trials, 63–67
memes, 82
Merchant, Nilofer, 190
message architecture, 223–24n6
metaphors, 138
Millionaire's Shortbread, 95–96, *97*
mistakes: learning from, 185–86;
    and vulnerability, 173–74
Moleskine, 29
Moore's Law, 15, 222n3
Morozov, Evgeny, 189
Morrell, Jennifer, 144–45
Mulaney, John, 131

National Institutes of Health (NIH),
    4, 29, 59, 63, 68, 212
National Library of Medicine, 63
Needotron, 116–17
Netflix, 111
The New York Times, 7, 158–59, *160*,
    161, 163, 166, 170
Newsom, Gavin, 176
NHS (National Health Service), 4,
    59, 77–78, 85, 212; Constitution,
    70; Service Manual, 4, 69;
    website, 69–70, *71*, 72–73
NIBRS (National Incident-Based
    Reporting System), 52–53
nominalization, 61
Norman, Don, 164
novelty, 14

Office of Naval Intelligence, 146
offline retailers, 44–45

offloading, 106
Old Navy, 8, 193–96, 201
online, shopping, 103, 106
Open to All, 194–95
organizations, evolving, 13

paragraphs, 66
passive voice, 60–61
Patagonia, 86, 106–7
Penzey, Bill, 167–68
Penzeys Spices, 7, 167–68, *169*, 193
phone sales, 101
pinkwashing, 170
Piron, Andre, *162*
plain language, 4, 78, 144
PLAIN (The Plain Language Action
    and Information Network),
    62–63
political statements, 167–68, *169*,
    170–71, 193, 234n4
positive writing, 25
Powell, Randy, 189–90
problems, framing, 75
producers/consumers relationship,
    158–59
proposals, 83
prototyping, 7, 29, 48, 181, 196,
    200–1
punchlines, 109

Qantas, 170, 171
Quesenbery, Whitney, 142–45

Race/Related, 159, 166
rapport-building, 21, 36, 42, 73, 164
recipes: media formatting of, 97–98.
    See also America's Test Kitchen;
    Cook's Illustrated

releasability, 149–50
research, 100–3, 165
Richards, Sarah, 111, 115, 120, 122,
    124–26, 221–22n1, 228n1
risk, embracing, 174–78
risk aversion, 60
roadmaps, 164, 198
Rollins, Henry, 233n1
Rongerude, Calla, 195–96

San Francisco Chronicle, 32
San Francisco Digital Services, 200
San Francisco's Bay Area Rapid
    Transit, 72
Sanders, Liz, 170
Santa Clara Public Health
    Department, 175–76
Sarkki, Kevin, 33, 224n7
Sasselov, Dimitar, 191, 192
second chances, 41–42
self-confidence, 77, 128
self-education, 137
Sessions, Robert, 225n2
Seth, Anil, 189
Shopify, 208
sidebars, 29, 48, 92, 99, 104,
    120, 122
silos, breaking out of, 29–31
simplification, 59, 131–32
skepticism, 1
Sleeping Giants, 206, 234n4
Snapchat, 140–41
social media, 96–97
The Spice House, 168
Sprockett, Shawn, 140–41
SRS (Summary Reporting System),
    52–53

Starr, April, 75–77, 136, 165–66,
    178, 211, 226–27n11
stock photography, 61–62
storytelling, 32
style guides, 23, 25; GDS, 124;
    Mailchimp, 22, 25–26; NHS,
    72–73
superbackers, 186

TED, 7, 134, 187–90, 191, 195, 201,
    208–9
TED.com, 188, 191, 192
TEDx, 189–90, 209
terrain simulators, 35
Terrett, Ben, 125–26
Tokyo, subway lines, 133
tone, 22, 27, 36; vs. voice, 20–21
touchpoints, 17, 23, 31, 33, 128
tradeoffs, 7, 70, 135–36, 135
transparency, 6, 42, 50, 207
Transport (typeface), 126
travelogues, 3, 28
trust, 139, 209–10; and confidence,
    83; earning, 50, 87, 127; and
    expectations, 125–26; implicit
    bargain, 203; and vulnerability, 8
truth, 132
Twitter, 111, 234n4
2D QR codes, 143, 145
typography, 72, 126–27

Uniqlo, 53
uniqueness, 32–33
UK government, 4, 6, 59, 68, 72,
    109–11, 112, 113–17, 118–19, 120,
    121, 122, 123
user-centered design, 6, 114–15

user-created content. *See* collaborative creation
user experience design, 128
user reviews, 31, 205

VAT (Value-Added Tax), 117, *118–19*, 120, *121*
Vibebot, 48, *49*
videography, 139–41
videos, Airbnb, 139–40
visual communication, 61–62, 85, 225*n*2
voice, 2–4, 6, 12; active vs. passive, 60–61; Banana Republic, 28–29, 35, 38; consistency in, 14, 17, 46; of the FBI, 52; at Mailchimp, 20, 23, 25, 208; visual aspects of, 12–13, 30; vs. tone, 20–21
volume, 5–6, 82, 208
voting, 142–44, *145*
vulnerability, 6–9, 154–55, 157, 161, 163, 170–71, 173, 180, 186, 200–1, 207–8

Wankbot, 47–48
warnings, oral vs. written, 66
Watzlawick, Paul, 134
weaknesses: acknowledging, 190; denying, 171; elevating, 4, 49–54, 57
Wilcox, Sara, 68, 72–73
Wodtke, Christina, 133–34, 138
World Information Architecture Day (2018), 148
Wurman, Richard Saul, 133–35

Yamanote Line, 133
Yuan, Eric, 197–200, 210–11

Zarzad Transportu Miejskiego (Warsaw), 72
Ziegler, Mel, 29, 31, 37
Ziegler, Patricia, 29, 31–33, 37
Zoom, 8, 197–200, 210
zoombombing, 198, 210
Zukowski, Deia, 104–5

About the author

MARGOT BLOOMSTEIN is one of the
leading voices in the content strategy
industry. She is the author of *Content
Strategy at Work: Real-World Stories
to Strengthen Every Interactive Project*
and the principal of Appropriate, Inc., a
brand and content strategy consultancy
based in Boston. As a speaker and stra-
tegic advisor, she has worked with marketing teams in a range
of the world's leading brands. The creator of BrandSort, she
developed the popular message architecture–driven approach
to content strategy. Margot teaches in the content strategy
graduate program at FH Joanneum University in Graz, Austria,
and lectures around the world about brand-driven content
strategy and designing for trust.

Colophon

SETAREH ASHRAFOLOGHALAI set the titles for this book in Benton Modern Display by Dyana Weissman and Richard Lipton, based on the Benton Modern text face originally designed by Tobias Frere-Jones and inspired by Morris Fuller Benton's Century Expanded. Frere-Jones designed Benton Modern for *The Boston Globe* and *Detroit Free Press*, institutions that have earned readers' trust in their own right. The body text of *Trustworthy* is set in Miller, which was designed by Matthew Carter. Newspapers and other forums of education around the world favor Miller and its variants to inform and empower their readers.